Deadly
Triangle

NEW
HORIZON
PRESS

Dear Reader,

We proudly present the newest addition to our internationally acclaimed true crime series of *Real People/Incredible Stories*. These riveting thrillers spotlight men and women who perform extraordinary deeds against tremendous odds: to fight for justice, track down elusive killers, protect the innocent or exonerate the wrongly accused. Their stories reveal the untold drama and anguish behind the headlines of those who face horrific realities and find the resiliency to fight back…

At Northeast Louisiana University in Louisiana, Ivrin Bolden Jr., a twenty-three year-old pre-medical student, his fiancée Joel Tillis and her teammate Brenda Spicer, who was rumored to be her lover, became embroiled in a bitter love triangle that ended in death. In *Deadly Triangle: A True Story of Lies, Sports and Murder* by Fran Parker, the lifeless body of Brenda Spicer was found in a dumpster on campus. A killer walked the streets and townspeople cried out for justice, but what unfolded was an incredible series of events, lies and escapes from the law that spanned across multiple states. Yet one woman, a native of Monroe, Louisiana, worked feverishly to uncover the truth behind the murders before another victim was claimed.

The next time you want to read a crackling, suspenseful page-turner, which is also a true account of a real-life hero illustrating the resiliency of the human spirit, look for the New Horizon Press logo.

Sincerely,

Dr. Joan S. Dunphy
Publisher & Editor-in-Chief

Real People/Incredible Stories

Deadly Triangle

A True Story
of Lies, Sports and Murder

By
Fran Parker

New Horizon Press
Far Hills, NJ

New Horizon Press
PO Box 669
Far Hills, NJ 07931

Parker, Fran. Deadly Triangle: A True Story of Lies, Sports and Murder

Cover design: Robert Aulicino
Interior Design: Susan Sanderson

Library of Congress Control Number: 2008927026

ISBN 13: 978-0-88282-340-9
ISBN 10: 0-88282-340-X

New Horizon Press books may be purchased in bulk quantities for educational, business or sales promotional use.
For more information please write to:
New Horizon Press
Special Sales Department
PO Box 669
Far Hills, NJ 07931
1-800-533-7978
Email: nhp@newhorizonpressbooks.com

www.newhorizonpressbooks.com
Manufactured in the USA

2013 2012 2011 2010 2009 / 5 4 3 2 1

To the Dead, we owe only truth.

—Voltaire

Author's Note

This book is based on the experiences of the author and reflects her perceptions of the past, present and future.

Information was gathered from court hearings and trials, court testimony, court documents, police reports and investigative files, prosecutors' files, press accountants, research and interviews in Arkansas, Louisiana, Tennessee and New Jersey.

In an effort to safeguard the privacy of certain people, some individuals' names and identifying characteristics have been changed. Certain quoted conversations attributed to characters are based on the recollections of witnesses, friends and families interviewed. Events involving the characters happened as described. Only minor details may have been altered.

Table of Contents

Prologue

The Northeast Louisiana State University custodian arrived at work by 7:00 A.M. to empty the trash and prepare the Science Building for classes. He hoped to leave work early, fish Black Bayou for bass until sunset and take his catch home for his wife to fry for supper.

He opened the door of the metal dumpster and at first glance thought the nude body stuffed within it was a mannequin—those fraternity guys playing tricks again. Then he saw a trickle of blood had dried beneath the pretty blonde's nose. Ants carrying crumbs trailed her tan legs. Trashed like a broken doll atop garbage bags, blue were her eyes fixed on the cloudless skies of March. Her bra was severed, her breasts exposed and her slacks were pulled down to her socks.

Shaking uncontrollably, the custodian yelled to a passing student, "Get the campus police. There's a body in this dumpster!"

Part 1

Monroe

Chapter 1
Phenomenal Luck

Along the university's quad, lined with moss-strung pin oaks, students rushing to Friday morning classes soaked up shafts of lemon sunlight between buildings. Six campus police cruisers lined the parking lot and a bevy of officers held students back.

Northeast Louisiana University Police Sergeant Ed Free, summoned from his Criminal Justice class, theorized that phenomenal luck had worked for and against the killer. "If the custodian had dumped the trash the night before, he might have discovered the body early and alerted us before the alibis were set into motion." And if he hadn't glanced inside the bin, a sanitation truck with a hydraulic lift would've compacted the load without examination. A killer had gambled that his victim would be ground into rubbish.

Although the University Police Department enforced campus ordinances, handled internal problems and quelled disturbances, major crimes were kicked up to the Monroe City Police Department. Detective Ricky Peel, a veteran investigator with a no-nonsense demeanor useful in questioning suspects, activated his siren while briefing his six-foot-three partner with curly copper hair, Detective Bill Causey.

"The caller said there's a body in a dumpster. Probably a laboratory cadaver or maybe a co-ed ditched an unwanted baby," Peel said.

A parking lot separated the crime scene from the two-story residence of the university president. The English-style house, built in the 1940s and painted the color of the yellow brick road of Oz, was surrounded by brick walls cushioning traffic sounds and rowdy students. Pink, white and watermelon azalea gardens relieved the rundown aura. The Northeast Louisiana University president, weighed down from deskwork and thinned by tennis with a low-key manner, became notified of the first murder in Northeast Louisiana University's fifty-three year history. Glue sniffing, marijuana, panty raids and streaking had accelerated to drug peddling, date rapes and violence.

A professor, at work in the computer laboratory, fretted over Joel Tillis, her prize pupil and protégé. The mood of Joel's boyfriend last evening nudged her peace. "Stick with him," she advised Joel during one of their breakups. "He's brilliant, has potential and will be a successful doctor."

Youthful passions and crises ebbed and flowed like a shifting tide. The ambitious Joel, of average intellect from a socially deprived background, was a teacher's reward—a slant soon to be cruelly altered. Paul Bannon, an administrator and athletic advisor, also felt undercurrents. "I was thinking of Joel, because I'd become afraid for her. She's a magnetic person and my wife and I had sort of adopted her during her four years of college." Verbal assaults from Joel's boyfriend during the previous evening's basketball game made Paul question why she tolerated the boyfriend—brainwashing, insecurity or misplaced love.

Paul's secretary burst in, "Campus security found a body. They think it's a Lady Indian." Chills rippled down Paul's arms. He raced downstairs and visualized Joel in the dumpster. Once Paul was informed the victim was most likely Brenda Spicer, Joel Tillis's friend and former basketball player for the Lady Indians, he felt he knew the motive and perpetrator. Duty bound to warn the NLU president, Paul pulled him aside, "Don't be surprised if the first name that surfaces is Ivrin Bolden."

"That's impossible. He's an honor roll student, serious and congenial from a prominent family. Why do you think that?" the NLU president asked.

"Let's talk privately. Not here." The same name seemed to be on a collective brain scan as news spread across campus.

Detective Bill Causey knelt beside the body. "I recognize this girl. She's on the Lady Indians basketball team. She came to our home for a cookout."

He wanted to throw his jacket over the young woman, but could not risk contaminating fiber evidence and instead scrawled notes. She was strangled, evident from the handprints and bruises around her throat. Contusions suggested a struggle. Her shirt was open exposing her breasts, white bra severed in the middle and slacks pulled down to her ankles with plaid socks and tennis shoes. She wore a gold bracelet with charms: a basketball, a unicorn, a four-leaf clover, a number thirteen, a tennis racket and a Magic Johnson caricature. There was a National Collegiate Athletic Association championship watch on the left arm.

Peel said, "That's odd. She was new to the team. I wonder whose NCAA watch she's wearing?"

Campus security briefed Causey on a missing persons report filed on Brenda Spicer after midnight, launching an all-night search by their graveyard shift. "Night duty officers alerted us of something that was off-key. The girl is a dropout last seen yesterday afternoon. By 11 P.M., the Lady Indians had panicked and were looking everywhere. Our officers were confused by the Amber Alert for a former student free to come and go at will. Joel Tillis, the missing girl's best friend and former teammate, seemed convinced something had happened to her and finally notified us. That white car across the street belonged to Miss Spicer. Miss Tillis had our officers open it and Tillis searched it. Thinking the car was hers, they wondered what she was looking for. Even stranger, when they gave up the search, we called Miss Tillis to meet us in front of the dorm and answer a couple of questions. A white car similar to the victim's entered the drive-way—turned out to be a student bringing his girlfriend home. Miss Tillis jumped into our patrol car, lay down on the back seat and ordered us to

'Lock it.' We asked why. She said, 'I thought it was someone else.' We figured she thought it was Miss Spicer. It scared the hell out of her and she didn't seem relieved by the possibility that her best friend was safe."

"I'll need a copy of that report," said Bill Causey. "We need to let Coach Doris Davies know she's one of her girls."

Causey took charge of his fifth murder investigation, a prime publicity case. He and Peel, former NLU basketball players themselves, had an inside track. Kim Cameron, a Lady Indian advisor, was close friends with Causey's parents.

"My gut tells me this will shake the foundation of our alma mater," said Peel. "Do you think we're too close to it?"

"You can't scratch your nose around here without poking a cousin or a friend in the eye. That might be a plus. Kim could be a valuable source of information."

Police photographer Charles Tullos stepped inside the dumpster for close-ups of bruises on the body's shoulders, handprints on inner thighs and a dialated rectum. Crime school training took over: "Think of L-stops, shutter speeds, angles. The body is an object; what gave it life is gone."

In the glove compartment of Brenda Spicer's car, Causey found a picture of Joel Tillis's boyfriend, Ivrin Bolden. He radiated aplomb, beamed as though he owned hotels on Yucatan. A sentimental greeting card and letter Ivrin had written to Brenda and signed with love gushed with clichés. It contained a puzzling double entendre, "I hope we can learn to SHARE Joel Tillis."

Chapter 2

Dreams and Nightmares

In the 1980s, Monroe, Louisiana, was a place of firsts and lasts. The highest concentration of millionaires per capita juxtaposed against the third highest poverty rate per capita in America, the cheapest place to retire and high on the list of most likely places to be murdered.

The first turf war in the "Land of the Sacred Silver Water," as the Ouachita Indians called their Eden, occurred when European soldiers of fortune canoed upstream from New Orleans and routed the peaceful tribe west. Then, during the Civil War, as President James Monroe's gunboat explored the mouth of the river, residents celebrated all night with bonfires, dancing and feasting. Fort Miro became Monroe.

The parish of rich Mississippi Delta soil is huddled in a valley where tornadoes skimmed over its green bubble dome of spread-oak canopies, hard oak forests and dank swamps. In this suppressed environment, the pastoral valley seemed safe, self-satisfied and detached from the outside world. Men with pioneering visions, energy and tall dreams penetrated the bubble. A local cropdusting operation outgrew spraying pesticide on grounded fields and soared beyond their wildest imagination. Their airline was named Delta, in honor of the rich, alluvial land that seeded its birth and it soon circled the earth.

Coca-Cola's first bottling plant was located in Monroe in 1912 when Joseph Biedenharn, the descendant of poor but industrious immigrants, inherited the patent from his uncle, Henry. The Biedenharn Gardens and Museum offer the world's only remaining nickel Coke machine.

In the 1960s, change seeped into the bubble. The general citizenry, subdued by the national spotlight on Southern bigotry, tried amending the sins committed by someone else's ancestors. Plantation Penitence, or the Delta Queen Syndrome, was a perpetual guilt trip foisted on the working class by heirs coasting on antebellum fortunes. Monroe prided itself on being the New South.

A film commissioner scouting movie locales marveled, "The region's a time warp of mansions, antiquities and rose gardens. Wooden T-cross telephone poles and electrical lines from the 1950s still string across main streets. Traffic stops and drivers pull to the curb for funeral processions." Fifty-six churches outnumbered gas stations and grocery stores. Religion and Republicanism anchored the population of 150,000.

Local wits referred to Old Line families and the nouveau riche as Crepes Suzettes, minorities as Soul Food and rural folks as Corn Pone. Intellect clashed with ignorance, sophistication with naiveté, the flavors a stew of European spice and Irish potato simplicity. Politics pervaded all levels. Even the lowest catfish inspector on the government rung prospered. Yet the tolerant New South was no longer amused or entertained by governors like Earl K. Long traveling cross-country on a shopping spree with stripper Blaze Starr or Cajun King Edwin Edwards indicted seventeen times before finally convicted of bribery in granting casino licenses.

Seldom acknowledged as such, Northeast Louisiana University was also a political entity, "A City Inside the City" pumping bucks and jobs into the economy. Billboards greeted visitors: THIS IS INDIAN COUNTRY. As the area's largest employer, adding 9,000 students and consumers to the tax base,

NLU had clout. "Seek the Truth" is chiseled in stone at the university entrance and emblazoned on diplomas and memorabilia, but the motto became irony with the murder of the former co-ed. Sports and education resided on opposite banks of Bayou DeSiard as competing adversaries—a separation that academicians found ironically appropriate. Two stadiums and an amphitheater climbed skyward in towering peaks, symbolizing millions spent annually in support of intense competitions. NLU sports gave citizens a unified cause to applaud. The games, generating profits and donations from alumni and Saturday night fans, were a core curriculum, the miracle glue of Monroe's hodgepodge collage. From September through June, the playing fields were a mega power plant electrifying the parish.

Long ignored and patronized by male-dominated athletics, the Lady Indians basketball team exemplified feminine achievement and racial tolerance. Feminism and race negated each other as did sport and race.

Sexual tolerance did not come as easily, though gays, if wealthy or chic, intellectual, accomplished or droll, were accepted. The town transvestite, a painter by day in overalls, worked evenings entertaining at lavish parties hosted by the jaded, preening in his red wig, sequined gowns or pink tutu.

When the Lady Indians basketball team rocketed to fame as the number two college team in the nation, the community reveled in glory. Sports analysts touted them to be number one the following year. In the rarefied atmosphere of the skybox atop the stadium, with its aerial view of campus and the heavens, patrons paid $1600 a year for amenities like an open bar and fried alligator hors d'oeuvres and celebrated the Lady Indians' triumph, a prize they would do about anything to keep.

Then, in a tragic scandal fated for six years of sensationalism and controversy, an extraordinary drama played out in complacent and mannerly Monroe. When the maelstrom settled and the truth emerged, the community suffered losses of innocence and trust in leaders, institutions and in each other. Unfortunately, however, this story could have happened anywhere where "Winning Is All."

Chapter 3

Unspeakable Acts

*L*ike the slow melting of icicles beneath a pallid sun, the painful stings of *summer bees, the knowledge of autumn stripping the earth and unspeakable acts killing innocence and trust, so the pain in a child's heart and soul is shaped.*

I was nine when I spent summer vacation with my aunt, uncle and cousins, sitting on their front porch, wishing someday dreams on the moon. By the faint light from a neighbor's house, two shadows circled and I heard a swishing sound and whimpering. I summoned my uncle, "A man on the road is whipping a lady with a switch."

My uncle, a strong and gentle giant, would help her, I thought. I tagged behind as he approached the black sharecropper and his wife who worked on an adjoining farm. She explained, "My folks live in town. It's lonesome out here. He won't let me go see 'em. I waited 'til he was asleep, tried to get to the highway and hitch a ride. He caught me."

My uncle told the man, "Well, you go on back to your place and take care of it there." *Physical pain was in my stomach: women are plow mules. Obey when the reins are pulled or be whipped.*

Years later, such memories drew me into the paths of two young women

11

with similar experiences. Brenda Spicer and Joel Tillis confided to teammates they had been sexually abused when they were young, vowing never to be violated or controlled again. A man viewing women as objects to be possessed would prove them wrong.

It was a South only Southerners know and understand. My mother, with a fifth grade education and children to support, divorced my abusive, alcoholic father, bought a bankrupt grocery store in a black neighborhood and realized for the first time that she was smart. Befriending customers and extending credit, the business flourished in an atmosphere of kindness and respect. She learned about customers' life stories, some heartbreaking. A battered woman came to the store with her arm in a cast. Sympathies come easy, actions harder. Mama bought a cot for the storage room and left a window unlatched for the woman to climb in and be safe from her husband's rage.

Then, there were two cots. A thirteen-year-old black boy, abandoned and living with reluctant relatives, was often hungry and whipped. The red blood clotted on his legs looked the same as mine. He ate free at Mama's store and she made him feel valued, "You can sleep here when you need to and guard the place for me." *Peanut, as his folks called him, became our little brother and each September, Mama bought his school clothes when she bought ours.*

The store burned, Mama retired and we lost touch with Peanut. She could no longer run a secret underground for the helpless and hide them in a safe place.

Two decades later, in my dress-for-success suit, as I left work, a group of men wearing yellow slickers lettered Public Works Department passed me. There was something vaguely familiar. Eyes don't change. I whirled around in the same moment he did. Mama had heard that while on a drunken spree his uncle had run him over with a truck. "Peanut! Dear God, is that you?"

"Miss Fran?" *We rushed to hug as his astonished co-workers watched, brother and sister again.*

"I've wondered about you so many times."

"Tell your mama I'm doing real well now. She's the sweetest lady, made me want to pay her back by doing better for myself."

He and Mama had somehow survived brutality with gentle hearts and

*grateful spirits. I planned never to be like her, too soft, giving too much of myself.
Instead, I became her clone.*

As a state probation officer, my husband supervised non-support offenders
and monitored the well-being of wives and children through home visits. When
his even-keeled nature waned to depression, I urged him to talk. "Every case is
the same: alcohol or drugs, violence and abuse, little education, poverty, cars
broken down and electricity disconnected. The wife of one of my
probationers called me. Her husband had bought a pretty dress their
ten-year-old daughter's size, hung it in the hallway and told her, 'You know
what you have to do to get this.' The mother came home from her waitress
job and the dress was gone. Her little girl wore it to school the next day. I
put the bastard in jail, but where does that leave his wife except a welfare
check that won't stretch. I feel like I'm putting band-aids on a levee break."

*We occasionally bought groceries for those caught in the bureaucracy of
approval for food stamps and welfare. My husband and I were alike in that
respect—soapboxers who gave the soap away and kept the box to stand upon.*

Chapter 4

Stinging Accusations

Assistant Coach Bryan Anderson waved to the lithe gods and goddesses of youth circling the giant belly of the coliseum in five-mile runs. Muscular and forty-something with a short haircut, he wore Northeast Louisiana University's standard maroon and gold uniform. Anderson was that rare breed who balanced competitiveness with harmony, a peacemaker who trained skilled players without outshining Head Coach Doris Davies. Six months ago, Brenda Spicer, or simply "Spicer", as coaches and teammates called her, had also been disciplined and absorbed in her game, light-hearted, popular and eager to please her coaches.

Davies had telephoned Anderson around 2:30 A.M., "Bryan, the team is in a damn uproar because Spicer didn't show up for the game. They pushed the panic button and called campus police. What do you suggest we do?"

"Doris, she might have gone home to Jena. Nothing to do but wait." He felt more concern for Joel, who regarded him as a father figure, and believed that her friendliness and generosity had sucked her into this huge mess not of her own making. He thought Joel was impressionable and Spicer difficult.

After a year of controversy following the NCAA win, coaching basketball had soured for Davies. In her forties, single and a heroine when winning, she was embittered by being made the fall guy for a series of messy dilemmas. How meteoric her professional rise before the slow-motion descent.

Around 1:00 A.M. and barely home from post-game interviews, Davies threw on sweats and intersected campus streets. She saw Brenda's car moistened by dew, parked near the Student Union Building and returned home exhausted but wide awake, her mind a shrieking warning whistle.

Her alarm clock buzzed at 7:00 A.M. sharp. Davies chose a navy suit, red silk blouse and navy pumps to wear that day. Trim, petite and tanned from outdoor basketball camps, she was attractive and likable in person, but television cameras and microphones accented her no frills style and drawl. She scowled under pressure and racked up penalties for arguing with referees, as did her male peers. Double standards infuriated her. Male coaches kicking butt, such as Bear Bryant, got hoisted from cheering fields. Her own remarkable record of bringing her team from obscurity to national stardom earned her such caustic labels as "hormonal." Davies slumped in her orange desk chair and dialed Joel's dorm.

Drained without sleep, Joel confronted her panic in the ingrained way she learned since childhood: sublimate above fear, get through it, survive it. Joel flinched at the strident ringing; it would be her boyfriend Ivrin or her mother calling to ask about Brenda again.

Davies asked, "Did she ever show up?"

"No, Coach. Campus security even unlocked the buildings. We checked hospitals and the main motels." Joel braced herself for another lecture, but Davies sounded restrained, "If she doesn't surface, come by my office after class."

Davies told Anderson, "Joel hasn't heard from her. After last night's sideshow at the game, we really don't need this brouhaha."

Campus police called. "Coach, the news isn't good. We found Brenda Spicer's body; she was evidently murdered." The walls shimmered in optical illusion. Anderson ignored the speed limit, driving Davies across the bridge. Buildings and landscape rolling by looked distorted in earthquake patterns.

In the jammed parking lot, she nodded curtly at the NLU president and told Detective Bill Causey, "I want to make a positive identification."

"The body bag is sealed, but I can show you our Polaroid shots." The fall and winter merged in nightmarish photographs. Davies focused on the NCAA watch on Spicer's arm, a giveaway.

The inconceivable, worse than feared, threatened to destroy her career. Her team's NCAA penalties and probation for sexual improprieties in recruiting the year before had been a mere sneak preview. The lid had popped off the scandal again.

The NLU president, his public relations staff and select colleagues fielded inquiries from reporters, parents and alumni. "This has to be a mistake," he said. Accusing the son of the Bolden family was a glasshouse on the San Madrid fault. With four post players graduating, Northeast Louisiana University was trying to recruit the Boldens' daughter and struggling to rebuild the team.

As an academician, the NLU president felt athletics played too exalted a role. Yet the realist, competing with six other state colleges for students, funding and alumni donations, conceded that sports ranked second.

He met with Davies who said, "I did receive a peculiar long distance call from Ivrin Bolden five weeks ago. He asked me to help him get his girlfriend back. I didn't know what he was talking about or what he thought I could do."

A private underground protected the Lady Indians. The official word was, "Answer what the police ask. Just tell the truth." The unwritten code needed no translation: Cooperate but don't volunteer. If you didn't see it, don't say it. We can't bring Spicer back. Careless talk can harm reputations.

Chapter 5

Under Pressure

For the usual Dress-Down Friday, Joel Tillis pulled on jogging sweats for an early class and psyched up to behave normally. A bad dream, this incorporeal terror—don't ever let them see you sweat—a rule applicable to game opponents and advice she gave Brenda Spicer on dealing with their coaches' pressures. "You can be friends, but not that close." She took a shortcut between high-rises, but didn't see the blue and white squad cars parked on the next street or somber students in clusters.

"After class," Joel recalled, "I was talking to a graduate assistant when I heard walkie-talkies in the hallway. I knew the radio static meant campus police." A runaway pulse pounded her ears, the static sounded like sirens wailing. She had a reason for speaking with the graduate assistant; he was about to become either alibi or accuser, depending upon his memory. Two uniformed policemen entered the graduate assistant's office. "Are you Joel Tillis?"

"Yes...I am." She avoided their eyes and studied the gold braiding on their Mountie hats.

"Would you come with us, please?" Joel hugged her textbooks in a praying hands stance and asked, "Did you find Brenda?" Overnight, she was calling her best friend by her first name instead of her nickname. Suspecting she knew the answer neither officer responded and they noticed she didn't ask where they were taking her.

"I guess it's bad, huh?" Joel asked.

"She's dead."

Gargantuan horror squeezed her legs to rubber. She thought of Brenda's zany humor and hunger for affection, their escapades and rebellions, vivid replays of her leaping to slam dunk a ball, her hair rising like an arrow trailing gold feathers.

"Since Miss Spicer was here visiting you, city police detectives need some information." Teammates who gave the police details opposed to Joel's learned what they had no desire to know. Their mentor in victories and losses who loaned them her last dollar, doled out aspirin, hauled them around in her car and kept watch on their grades began to change when Brenda Spicer died. Had she actually changed? Had they really known her or were there two Joels?

In Joel's dorm room, Detective Bill Causey showed Joel a photo, "Can you tell us who this is?"

"My boyfriend. I…I left it in Brenda's car."

"We need to look through anything that belonged to her."

She pointed at Brenda's overnight bag in the closet.

Karin Blue, a teammate on the Lady Indians, spoke of Brenda's despondency the day before as she reviewed the file box of cards and letters kept in Joel's room that had vanished as though imagined. "No, I don't know where any letters are," said Joel.

Then, an inconceivable twist occurred. Fifteen hours had elapsed since the victim had disappeared and her body found, yet no one had notified her parents that she was missing—much less dead. While busy stomping out fires, no one had thought of it. In the small town of Jena, the sheriff and townspeople knew Brenda Spicer's parents and Northeast Louisiana

University's student records had emergency contact numbers.

Troubled over Brenda's depression, her mother tried reaching Brenda at home, then dialed a familiar number, "Joel, is Brenda there?"

An intake of breath—something incoherent—then Joel whispered to Detective Ricky Peel, "It's Brenda's mother."

"You haven't told her?"

Joel listened with her back turned. Peel placed the receiver against his temple and formulated his words. "Mrs. Spicer, this is Detective Ricky Peel with the Monroe Police Department. Something has happened to your daughter. I'm sorry. She's gone. They found her body this morning. Foul play is indicated. When can you get here?"

The deepest fears of Brenda's mother materialized. Her voice echoed from a wind tunnel, "Her father and I can be there this afternoon." She called her husband and three children living out of state. Their oldest daughter adored Brenda and they exchanged newsy letters with sunny quotes. Brenda couldn't have died, Mrs. Spicer later said in our interview, not her child, not the ponytailed adolescent doing flips off the diving board, the gifted athlete, the stubborn teenager resisting guidance.

When the detectives left, Joel called her mother, "Brenda was found murdered and the police want a formal statement from me." In turn, Joel's mother called Ivrin Bolden in New Orleans, an odd person to notify since she had witnessed his angry scenes and his rage at Brenda. Yet Joel said his name kept popping up as the last known person to have seen her alive.

Kim Cameron, an NLU athletic advisor, received a call from her mother at work, "I heard on the radio that a murdered girl was found on campus and her identity's being withheld."

"Oh dear God, it has to be Brenda! Everyone was looking for her last night. He's finally killed her."

Detectives summoned Jason Santz, a former boyfriend of Brenda's, from class. The memories engulfed him. Brenda had told him of Ivrin's demands to break off her friendship with Joel or Ivrin would handle it. Santz regretted his parting joke, "What's he's going to do, kill you?" They had laughed about it. Though his saunter and build stamped him as a baseball jock, Santz was also a Renaissance man who enjoyed literature. He and Brenda, athletic, scholarly and sensitive, had much in common.

Santz told Peel, "I saw her before she dropped out of school. She said she was having problems with Coach Davies and the basketball team that she needed to sort out."

"Can you be more specific about the problems?"

"Sure. Brenda said Davies thought she and Joel Tillis were gay; their friendship wasn't good for the team or the school. Brenda said she was quitting NLU; the situation was too complicated and heating up. Ivrin had written her a letter saying he'd do anything to get his girlfriend back and threatening her if she didn't stay away from Joel."

His voice cracked and Santz averted his eyes, "I wanted to talk to the jerk, but she didn't want to involve me."

Detectives read the missing person report. "Joel Tillis stated, 'Brenda dropped me at the coliseum at 5:45 P.M. and was going back to the dorm to change clothes.'" Joel's account didn't fit. Suite mates said Brenda showered, dressed and did her hair and makeup before leaving around 4:00 to meet a mystery caller.

In a beehive of activity at the athletic offices, the coaches called a team meeting. Openly weeping, the players huddled into their jackets as though winter had returned and vented among themselves. One player said, "Spicer stepped around bugs on the sidewalk. She was a helpless kid playing in the big league."

The staff instructed the team, "You're going to be under a lot of pressure, but don't make any comments to the press. Hang tough, conduct yourselves as a team." Terror sealed their lips. Those without reason to fear exposure of their private lives feared the name whispered down the lineup.

"The reporters stalked us," said Lady Indians teammate Sara Pollard, "with remote vans, television cameras and photographers stationed outside our dorm entrances." In the circus atmosphere, athletic supporters housed players until the furor subsided. Frightened parents ordered their children home. Tension gripped the community. Classes seemed like afterthoughts. The staid old buildings and lazy bayou seemed to curtain some lost Twilight Zone. Lectures on arts, philosophy and history droned in the ears of the young sensing no practical application to their precarious world.

Coach Davies called Detective Bill Causey, "I want to bring Joel Tillis and teammate Wendy Ballard to the police station regarding something Brenda Spicer told them a while back."

A customer mentioned the radio bulletins about a murdered girl to a service station owner. "She'd been missing since yesterday evening. The cops found a picture of a black guy in her car." The owner, who also oversaw the mini storage units across the street, thought of the odd occurrence the day before near unit #104 and looked up the records: leased to an Ivrin Bolden Jr. He called the police, "I may have information about the murdered girl."

Joel, Wendy and the coaches were ushered into Causey's office. Joel managed to sidetrack Wendy from her snap judgment about Ivrin's involvement and said, "Brenda was raped by three guys in her freshman year and by another male after the attack.

"Brenda had several boyfriends, she also dated another guy who attends college in Arkansas. And she talked on the phone with another man." Causey wondered why Tillis was pointing fingers. He suspected the story of the service station attendants seeing a mixed race couple at the warehouse had made the rounds.

Joel recounted that Brenda called her in Jena on the previous Monday, "She was alone, so after practice I drove there and stayed overnight. About 2 A.M., the doorbell rang. Just Brenda's brother." It would be another interview before she told detectives about Brenda summoning her because of harassing telephone calls, that when she arrived, Brenda lay on the den sofa with her pistol nearby.

Joel suggested a spurned suitor or rapist who had returned as viable suspects. Causey noticed she hadn't mentioned the sticky conflicts with Ivrin Bolden.

Causey looked at Coach Davies, "I need to meet with you privately."

Joel and Wendy waited in the reception area.

"Is there anything else you can tell me?" Davies asked.

"Well, Ivrin Bolden was the last person we can determine who might have seen her alive." Causey made a note to track down those involved in the rape.

Joel's mother imagined her sacrifices and hopes in a twisted heap. Snippets of overheard conversations left luminous trails. Ivrin's fake sorrow on the phone, his entreaties that she help him, his insinuations that the cops might make too much of his and Joel's and Brenda's little spats slithered in her mind.

Chapter 6
Unnerving Meetings

While Joel hedged questions in the back wing of the police station, Brenda's father told the desk clerk, "Detective Bill Causey is expecting us."

Causey answered the buzzer and told Joel, "Brenda's parents are up front." He studied her response: momentarily jolted, nervous at the prospect of seeing them, a bit defiant, no condolences. "You don't want to talk to them? Okay, you can wait here if you'd be more comfortable."

Brenda's parents listened to details but kept their emotions private. In contrast to the Northeast Louisiana University big wigs who would come to the police station to meet Ivrin and his parents for his interview, no one from NLU met the Spicers at the station. They came and went quietly.

Causey asked Joel, "Since your boyfriend was the last known person to see Miss Spicer, could you call and ask him to return and answer a few questions?" Expecting the request, Ivrin borrowed a car and left his at the home of Joel's mother.

Ivrin honed his explanations and alibis, his wrath kicked into road rage as he whipped in and out of traffic. Joel would cover herself but what about him? Joel was frantic and accusatory on the telephone and had already partially spilled her guts. If the cops turned up the burner, she could blow like a hot air balloon. Ivrin was angry and most likely thought that Joel had alienated him from his family, sabotaged medical school and his reputation.

Recalling when Ivrin arrived at the front desk of the police station, an officer said, "He stormed into the station yelling, 'The Lady Indians are a bunch of lesbians! Joel Tillis and Brenda Spicer are gay and I'm being set up!'"

Causey ushered Ivrin into a room and asked, "Did you return to your warehouse after cleaning it out earlier? And does anyone other than you and Joel Tillis have keys to it?"

"No."

"You said you never left the coliseum during the Lady Indians' game, but football player Zachary Gil says he passed you running across the bridge at halftime. Where were you going?"

"Yeah…I forgot. Joel had left a pair of tennis shoes from storage in my car. She told me to run to her dorm and get them before the girl she'd promised them to had left. Joel's mother's high heels were hurting her feet, so I brought the car back." The tennis shoe run served two purposes: to muddy Gil's account of why and when he saw Ivrin run across the bridge and to explain how Joel's car got to the coliseum.

"Would you allow us to search your warehouse and your car and are you willing to take a lie detector test? Based on our information, you're a suspect. The searches and the PSE test could possibly clear you."

"I'm not making any more statements or signing any waivers until my mother and our attorney arrive." Ivrin agreed to return Sunday evening with legal representation.

As Ivrin and his mother exited the police station, Causey trailed behind and heard Ivrin's mother ask, "Where's your car?"

"It wasn't running right. I left it in Hammond and borrowed one." Following his mother to Shreveport for talks with their lawyer, Ivrin made mental notes to rehearse with Joel about the tennis shoe errand.

Dispatched to Hammond, Detective Jim Gregory of the Crime Unit told Police Chief Willie Buffington, "If I saw four cops shaking down my car, I'd be a little worried. He stood in the carport with Joel's mother, laughing and joking. His car had been wiped clean and vacuumed of prints and fibers."

Causey and Peel worked the weekend reviewing witness statements to pinpoint contradictions. "If Tillis is the nurturing Mary Poppins everyone claims, maybe she's afraid of him. Let's bring her in again and see if we can tap that fear."

The austere neon corridors of the police station reeked of pine scented floor wax and chicory coffee. Masculine odors of shaving lotion and leathered holsters alerted Joel to the risks. "I'll be happy to help you in any way I can," she told Causey. Her angled head and contemptuous smile said otherwise.

Exasperated by her jousting, Peel said, "On Friday night, Mr. Bolden walked in here yelling that you and Brenda Spicer and the basketball team are gay. If you'd seen how wild he acted, you would know to be afraid. He hates women; he hates you; he fits the profile of someone who will kill again." Joel faked a yawn. Ivrin had warned her about their tricks. They could not fathom all she would lose by going against him. He would never harm her, for she knew how to manage him.

Causey switched on the tape recorder, "Okay, we need to clear up certain elements surrounding the disappearance of Brenda Spicer." He was convinced that Ivrin had moved the body at halftime, but needed to refute his story without tipping off Joel.

"Did you mention anything to him about getting something for you?" Causey asked.

Not catching on, she answered nonsensically. "No. No. I didn't… because she said that ah…Brenda said, 'I was waiting for somebody,' so I knew she wasn't there."

He tried another angle, "During halftime, did Ivrin leave the stadium?"

Communications had improved overnight. Later, in written form, she corroborated the tennis shoe run. For good measure, she had enlisted the help of her roommate and teammate, Karin Blue. "Well…uhm…I had promised someone a pair of sneakers from storage and asked Ivrin to go and get them. That's why he left the coliseum."

"How long was Ivrin gone before he returned?"

"Well, I'll say about fifteen to twenty minutes."

Causey noted that Ivrin had said he was away maybe five minutes or so.

"Okay, did he bring you the tennis shoes?"

"No…well, he gave them to my roommate Karin, but the girl I was giving them to…uhm…had already left with her family. So therefore, since Karin is also from the same town, she'll take them on her next trip home."

"Miss Tillis, during the search for Brenda Spicer, you and your roommate drove to the warehouse twice. What did you expect to find there?"

"I didn't know. Since Brenda earlier said the warehouse, I didn't know if they had a…you know, a gift there. So I went back to check and didn't find anything." The detectives concealed their disgust. With her best friend missing, she claimed to be looking for a present?

On Sunday evening, when Ivrin returned to the station with his parents, his sister and two Shreveport lawyers along with two Monroe lawyers on standby, he had mellowed to a model citizen ready to clear up a terrible mistake.

Police officers were surprised to see Celebrity Night at the station. The NLU president, Coach Davies, Assistant Coach Anderson and his wife and Joel Tillis were among the cast greeting or introducing themselves to the Boldens. Police Chief Larry Ellerman was there in regards to the crime.

Detective Ricky Peel asked Bill Causey, "So where's their Spirit of Today marching band and the dance squad?"

Chapter 7

Shocking Headlines

*O*n *March 5, 1987, the newspaper headline glared: MURDERED GIRL FOUND IN CAMPUS DUMPSTER. In the yearbook picture, eighteen-year-old Brenda Spicer wore a tailored blouse and sweater with a string of pearls, the attire of a sorority pledge at a welcoming tea. Far from that, she was a district basketball star and a former Lady Indian point guard. A classmate was quoted,* "Brenda was always head of the class in grades, vivacious, friendly and upbeat. She had no enemies."

She had at least one, I thought. Soon, street talk murmured that she had carried a gun and was being terrorized. I sensed there was more to her story. Sitting in my sunroom, I watched a blue heron wade the bayou behind my home. A Muskogee duck pecked at a mallard, driving him from the shallows—the strong preying on the weak. My own children were grown and gone. I love young people and abhor cruelty and intolerance.

My life was at a crossroads: I was forty-two, recently widowed and disillusioned with my career as a political spin doctor. Doing public relations for so long, I could wet my finger and test the wind for underlying motives beneath the rhetoric. Weary of working the wings of powerful and ambitious politicians' dreams, my rubber soul had bounced back to its verity.

The newspaper article became the impetus for a six-year journey—bizarre delvings into twisted, disheartening and even dangerous psychologies. Tracking the truth and uncovering the betrayals and subterfuge turned into a mission.

Chapter 8

Vials
of Blood

Ivrin's lawyer directed him to sign the search waivers and submit hair samples. Two vials of blood for typing, drug and alcohol screening and saliva and secretor compatibility went to the State Crime Laboratory.

Afraid Ivrin might bolt if tape-recorded, Detective Bill Causey made notes: "Stated that around 4:15 P.M. on Thursday, March 5, he and Joel Tillis returned to Harris Hall where he stayed in the lobby until about 5:00 P.M., then left and drove to the Student Recreation Hall and played video games. Around 5:30 P.M., stated he saw Brenda Spicer's car at an intersection, waved her down and got Joel Tillis's camera from her. Stated he drove to a store and paid a little over five dollars for film to a white female in her forties working the camera department. Suspect said he returned to the dorm around 6:00 P.M., walked to the game with Joel Tillis's mother and several others."

Hooked to the lie detector, better known as Detective Jimmy Zambie's *never-lie-to-your-mama machine*, Ivrin failed two psychological stress evaluations. Zambie told Chief Buffington, "He lit up. The graph lines are typical textbook examples of untruthful answers."

The Boldens' attorney told Causey, "I've recommended he not talk to you any further." The detectives wouldn't get another shot at their suspect.

A Northeast Louisiana University coach hosted the team for Sunday night supper to drop their defenses away from curiosity seekers. Joel, weeping and binging, told the group, "I know he killed her. I'm afraid of him. I never want to see him again."

Joel meant her declarations for the moment and Ivrin meant his. They came down to what was later said to be, "It's your call, babe. We stick together or go down together. I'll broadcast everything about you and Spicer and the Lady Indians. Nobody's gonna believe her death was a big shock to you."

Brenda's funeral was moved from the Catholic Church to the high school gymnasium to accommodate the crowd and mounds of overflowing flowers. A friend memorialized her, "High on life, she was spirited and generous, extremely bright and color-blind. Always the star, in the game for the joy of playing and without conceit. A smile that lit up a room, an infectious laugh and a quiet serious side, with love of family, curiosity for learning, steadfast loyalty and generosity toward those who had less." Jason Santz's emotions ran the gamut from pain to anger. Joel's shell cracked; devastated, she wept for the first time since the murder.

Chapter 9

In the Beginning

B renda Spicer thrashed to wakefulness—eighteen and safe in the athletic dormatory, not fifteen and still living at home. Nightmares often replayed the football game when she was cornered in the bathroom behind the bleachers. The light flipped off to ink-like darkness as smells of urine, Clorox and cheap aftershave hung in the air. She felt the humiliation and powerlessness of the moment, as her cashmere sweater, plaid skirt and soul were stripped away as bodies heaved on top of her. Her pleading protests answered by guttural laughter and obscenities uttered like love. In the kind oblivion of leaving her body, she felt her desire dry inside as semen and her shame harden to hatred. Afraid she might die, she ceased fighting, willed her senses to the field beyond and the crowd cheering the maleness of block and kick, pummel and shove.

The industrious Spicer family all played piano, had hobbies, a menagerie of pets and installed a swimming pool, play equipment and a fence to corral their offspring. Brenda's privileged life tagged her for happiness. Town recreation centered on sports and in the fourth grade, she discovered basketball. Her coaches recognized her natural talent, absorption and willingness to work. Hoops in her bedroom and bathroom were the normal décor, and she saw the Globetrotters play on tour. By junior high, she had earned district stardom with "Brenda Leads Jena" a frequent headline.

Curious and congenial, whether chatting at the park square or scoring the most points in a game, Brenda belonged to the town. She was never at a loss for conversation and related well to adults and other athletes eager for pointers. "Age, color and race didn't matter," said friends. "People were her oxygen."

In the seventh grade, Brenda wrote her first protest paper. On a vacation, her brother caught a large bass with a perch lodged whole in its mouth. Disturbed, she questioned the symbiosis of survival, the pecking order of white over black, male above female, human over animal.

She could not comply with attempts to convert her from tomboy to belle. Her mother worried about Brenda's single-minded interest in sports, and for an Old South prom, she designed and sewed a peach taffeta dress with puff sleeves and a sash. When she posed for snapshots with a dubious expression, Brenda told her prom date, "If you dare laugh, I'm outta here."

Issues of sexism and racism intermingled inexorably with athletics and her circle of friends. She abhorred intolerance and mock romances contrived to mollify society. "If someone could throw a ball and hit the hoop," said her mother, "Brenda respected them. She disliked the underdog structure."

Schools and sports heavily integrated; for dating or social functions, young people were expected to stick with their own. The Spicers welcomed both races for barbecues and swimming. Two of those friends would have their names tossed into those under suspicion.

Some people in Jena cheered Brenda while criticizing her for socializing with blacks off the sports fields. She identified with the lyrics of a Meg Smith song, "I'd have probably found this trouble even without my Southern home…"

If she played fair, life would be a paradise of high priced sneakers, designer shorts and winning seasons. Then everything spun out of control, shaking her self-esteem. The general attitude about the rape varied from, *I don't believe you…Unless you can positively identify them, what can be done about it?…What did she expect hanging around with black guys?*

Traumatized, she tried to live down the notoriety. Peers she had treated kindly had viciously raped her and some of her white friends acted as though she had invited the assault.

She always carried a wad of cash from her beloved father, bought teddy bears for friends and treated them to movies and meals. While collecting inspirational poems, Brenda played basketball with vengeance and grew independent. One female trainer became her comfort. Coaches were goddesses worshipped, obeyed and imitated. Brenda lashed out at her mother's counsel.

Her world narrowed to athletics and the circle of women always training and competing. Many of them shared her dilemma of suppressed passions and societal demands and became her second family—a consoling sisterhood. On the court, nothing could stop her, but her three all-district championships and Most Valuable Player awards did not heal the wounds.

After graduation, Brenda spent the summer close to her father, who helped her shop for her college wardrobe and bought her a new car. Brenda's mother urged her toward a business major and she reluctantly enrolled in accounting at Northeast Louisiana University. In decisions that might have saved her life, she bypassed scholarships from other colleges to follow her dream of playing for the Lady Indians basketball team.

The night before she left for college, a guy she had dated briefly rang the doorbell. She had heard he was getting married very soon. Circling a hole in the concrete driveway with the toe of his boot, he lifted her chin, "I love you. Give me one reason not to do it and I won't."

"Naaw, you're sweet to ask, but I'm too young to turn into a baby factory and be stuck here."

Joel Tillis's parents had divorced when she was seven. Raising three daughters on her own was tough on Joel's mother and money was tight. Working several jobs, her struggles and her sadness hung perpetual guilt on Joel, who ached to make her mother smile again. Even when she married again and life became easier, her oldest daughter still felt she had dues to pay. As the first black girl to play Little League on a boys' team, she learned acceptance as a people pleaser. That was fourteen years ago and she was still trying to keep the peace and make everybody happy.

A six-foot tall senior, Joel was gap-toothed in the attractive trademark way of Madonna and model/actress Lauren Hutton, a one-woman cheering squad with intoxicating energy. Her offbeat humor and Earth Mother warmth won popularity and friends laughingly dubbed her "Martha White" for the popular baking flour.

Criminologists say, "Killers are not born, they are made, clinging to the knees of their parents." In his New Orleans apartment, Ivrin awoke to sweat drenching his T-shirt. Joel told friends about his memory of being whipped with an extension cord for some minor infraction.

In group pictures, Ivrin riveted the eye, planted like the blood red rose in a Salvador Dali painting to draw in the viewer. As a Northeast Louisiana Unversity freshman, his six-foot-six height, impeccable taste in clothing and magnetic aura distinguished him in a crowd. Then his Honor Society photos gradually regressed from smiling studio poses to before-and-after shots of morose frowns. By junior year, he looked frazzled, overloaded and contentious.

Ivrin's father had labored and provided, took gambles to get ahead, banked money and learned to play golf. Moving to an affluent suburb, the Boldens left their modest beginnings behind.

Though basking in his family's bucks and brashness, Ivrin seemed connected to them only by their liberal support of his becoming a doctor. Nothing else in their hoity-toity exceed and excel environment appealed and nothing he did seemed good enough. Any grade below an A resulted in angry scenes and punishments. Undaunted by his aloofness, they pushed his luminary qualities.

When Ivrin got into trouble, a psychologist observed, "Can you imagine what his parents would do if he spilled his milk?"

A fraternity brother said, "We were delegates to Boys State for government and political study—not my forte. Ivrin sensed I disliked it and made me feel comfortable. I thought, *what an okay guy*. His stature and personality shouted leader. His link to a murder knocked me out. I argued, 'No way. It's frame-up.'"

But the fellow-well-met often exhibited a flipside. Some spotted disquieting arrogance and coercion when manipulation failed. A faculty sponsor said, "One of our Scholastic Mortar Board students mispronounced his first name and he whittled him down like the guy walked on all fours."

In his high school senior year, Ivrin's yearbook featured eleven photographs of himself and he showed no discomfiture over such excessive notice. As school mascot, he wore an indian chief ensemble of a feathered headdress, tribal fetishes, fringed vest, buckskin pants and moccasins. Hands reaching skyward, he communed with the Great Spirit. In another picture, he gripped a diminutive male teacher in a headlock with a raised tomahawk.

Winning every prize easily was a perpetrated myth. He and a female rival had dogged each other's heels scholastically since ninth grade. By April of their senior year, based on grade point averages, the Shreveport Times listed her as valedictorian and Ivrin as salutatorian. Second place unthinkable, his parents made sure the school corrected the mistake before graduation. After being allowed to take an extra eight-week math and science course, his two A's counted a few hundredths of a percentage point and edged him ahead.

A school counselor reflected, "Sometimes very bright, prosperous people feel the rules don't apply to them."

When Ivrin ignored the rules, consequences appeared to be covered. An old rumor was, "A girl he dated in high school vanished and he was a suspect. Finally labeled a runaway, nothing came of it and it wasn't publicized because legally he was a minor." The story surfaced again after Brenda's murder.

When Ivrin first took Joel to meet his parents, she described their house as, "So posh I was afraid to sit on the furniture. His parents and his sister came home and went straight to their bedrooms, leaving us alone in the den." Based on the past, they may have brushed Joel off from wariness of him getting too thick with any girl—and a country girl at that.

Ivrin's mother, admiring Joel's gold chain, remarked, "We gave Ivrin a chain just like that." Seething, Joel countered, "This is not Ivrin's chain. My mother bought it for me." Gold chains, as proof of how spoiled Ivrin was, often surfaced in Joel's conversations, "We had a tennis date and he pulled off his expensive crossweave chain and laid it on the ground. When he missed it, he didn't even go back and look for it. A male high school instructor and a male college professor also bought him jewelry."

Joel railed at the Boldens' suggestion she was mercenary and kept Ivrin in a tug-of-war with his family. Slighted, she enjoyed his largesse while pushing his independence from them.

In Shreveport, a second rumor endured that before Joel, another girl Ivrin dated was roughed up without charges filed. Tales of vanished or scuffed females were hush hush. ·

College freed him of parental supervision. One close friend had a slender build, light skin and effete features. Ivrin added extras to his dorm room—a small refrigerator and high tech stereo system. Reserves Officers' Training Corps earned him an Army scholarship to medical school and a military commission before going into practice.

His general reputation at Northeast Louisiana University was affable and he bought six cartons of orange juice each morning in the cafeteria. The cashiers made a joke of it and nicknamed him O.J., a prophetic vision coming a decade before former football star O.J. Simpson was charged with two murders.

Without time for team sports, Ivrin transferred his competitive nature to cutthroat recreation. Joel said, "He's the only person I know with a monogrammed table tennis racket and who simply keeps playing until he wins." A Lady Indian observed, "Losing at pool once threw him into a rage and he snapped the cue stick in two. A silly game, but it said a lot about him."

Temper also surfaced when he encountered grade problems. "He was so terrified of his parents," said Joel, "that in a pre-med course he had the choice of an A on the test and a C in the class or split it down the middle with two B's. Knowing a C would infuriate his folks, he opted for the two B's."

After he scored poorly on another examination, Ivrin explained his heavy schedule to his professor. Though sympathetic, the professor refused to change the grade. The professor recalled that Ivrin waited in the parking lot, trailed on the professor's bumper for five miles and parked in his drive-way, where Ivrin may have been thinking, *I know where you and your family live.*

A female professor teaching advanced math sized him up differently, "Smart, not brilliant. When the amount of time required became obvious, he dropped my class. I think he avoided situations he couldn't master."

A graduate assistant allegedly showed leniency and gave Ivrin an A.

A repulsed football player said that he was also offered an A and cooperated with police by wearing a wire to tape another overture.

A glossy Lady Indian poster of Joel Tillis in body-hugging spandex, full lips pouting, long legs apart irked Ivrin. He spent weekends in Monroe, where he rented a room at a fancy hotel. She resented his power over her life.

On their two-year anniversary of dating, Ivrin had rented a private yacht to cruise the Gulf with a tuxedoed waiter serving champagne, shrimp cocktails and chateaubriand to just the two of them.

Ashore, Joel broke the romantic mood by calling a friend, Cherise Gates, to prattle about their Camelot date. Ivrin protested, "You two can't even part your hair different or pick a movie without the other's opinion. You let your friends horn in."

"Since high school, Cherise and I vowed we'd be like Oprah Winfrey and Gayle King—skin tight, each other's sounding board and advisor."

"Yeah, well you advise her not to ruin our evening that maxed out my credit card." His parents had put him on an allowance.

Along with romance troubles, the psychological banging of his high chair widened the breach from his family. On school records, he listed Hammond as his hometown and listed Joel's mother as his "mother and next of kin in an emergency."

In lucid moments, Joel wanted out and used his possessive jealousy as revenge and a weapon. Their arguments and breakups in the spring and summer before his graduation set the stage for the fall semester when Brenda Spicer became Joel's ultimate retaliation.

Joel still struggled for passing grades and remained in Monroe to attend summer school while Ivrin prepared his move to New Orleans. Ivrin called Joel's mother with a plan, "I'm taking a summer class at LSU in Baton Rouge. Since you live so close, could I stay with you until September?"

Joel couldn't object without revealing the problems between them. Living with her family might solidify his hold until her anger cooled. As a bonus, his parents would be royally ticked. The arrangement irritated Joel. Rivalry had always surged between them and her clan of fun-loving, laidback relatives were a part of his attraction. Teaching her mother to build a hydrogen bomb in the kitchen seemed simpler than explaining his Jekyll and Hyde sides and their cold war.

On trips home, Joel accepted dinner out or a movie, but the stalemate prevailed. In September, Ivrin settled into his New Orleans apartment and she welcomed incoming freshman Brenda Spicer to the athletic dorm.

Their conflicting desires—Joel making it big in business or as a television sportscaster, Brenda coaching and moving to wherever Joel worked and Ivrin becoming a wealthy physician and marrying Joel—jeopardized it all.

Chapter 10

Poignant Flashbacks

College often felt large and lonely. The older players watched over Joel, forging friendships within their circle, changeable with new semesters, new seasons and new players. She fell discreetly in step with the Lady Jock world of freedom and sophistication.

Joel Tillis and Ivrin Bolden had gravitated toward each other, friends at first, dating occasionally and then going steady. Before Joel, he had dated a girl who had a child and struggled financially. She milked his tendency to buy affection and actually slapped him when they argued. Onlookers said, "He didn't seem violent then or else he held himself back. Instead of swapping blows, he'd cry about it."

Joel's friends laughed when she first brought him around, "Be serious, girl. Short shorts or skinny funky pants with cowboy boots?" Rebellion against the fastidious dress code imposed at home was temporary. Vogue could be bought and Joel made him over by selecting a trendy wardrobe.

Commanding attention, the attractive couple, taller than their peers, seemed an ideal balance. Yet their romance puzzled some. Ivrin, handsome and wealthy, though peculiar at times and a loner, could have dated a campus beauty with polish. Joel, with her rough edges, was pretty but no enchantress. Part of Ivrin's attraction seemed her popularity and capacity for fun that brought out the Saturday side of his goal-oriented nature. In turn, his studious, systematic habits steadied her impulsiveness.

Friends speculated, "I think they gave each other security and societal approval."

Joel marveled at his affluence. They took weekend trips to amusement parks; he bought her a new computer, jewelry, whatever she wanted. They often behaved more like study pals impressing the dormatory proctor, "Whenever I checked, they were always studying with the television and radio off. Ivrin's room was immaculate."

Joel's effervescent side created ripples. Accustomed to the spotlight himself, he felt diminished by her acclaim as a forward guard and her time and attention to others rubbed. She couldn't be tamed. During spring recruitment, she hopped on a golf cart and drove around campus promoting Northeast Louisiana University to potential students and their parents.

Ivrin's smile cracked easily. Beneath his surface of courtesy and compulsion for order, Joel spotted control and complexity. Their quarrels ended with inevitable making up and a love-hate element seeped into their addiction. One student became embroiled inadvertently. "Joel helped us in the box office with ticket sales. We visited and joked around while we worked. Ivrin dropped by and got in my face, 'Why are you always talking and laughing with her? Stop crowding my girlfriend.'"

Joel discerned that beyond amorous jealousy, Ivrin envied her, withheld praise for game victories and ferociously competed with her, more adversary than lover. Friends sensed she found the drama of a boyfriend blowing fuses in public flattering.

"I can't help it. Your devoting so much time to others drives me crazy."

When Joel took him to Hammond on weekends, she awed family and friends with his imposing credentials, "After graduation, he's going to medical school." Her sister figured him "Too Tidy Bowl nice and scrubbed up perfect," reeking of cologne, sampling food, praising her mother and scrubbing pots.

Soon they visited Hammond sporadically. Confiding deep resentment of his parents prodded him to surpass all classmates and engineered his personal life. He seldom went home and steered Joel toward less reliance on her family.

Kim Cameron warned her, "There's something odd about a guy who never sees or calls his parents until he needs money."

Joel told him, "I'm not staying away from my folks because you don't like yours." He bonded with her boisterous country clan. Joel's mother encouraged him to show patience during Joel's tantrums. This week's squall was next week's surfing wave and anesthetized her to the undercurrents.

Though his excesses and exuberance for their family life struck Joel's mother as peculiar, she warmed to her daughter's good fortune. "Like an excited kid, Ivrin anticipated the holidays and special occasions we celebrated. He said in a wistful way, 'We don't do that at my house.' He loved Mardi Gras and New Year's Eve in New Orleans. During birthday parties, he ran around in a party hat blowing a roll-up horn. On Christmas morning, he banged on our bedroom doors at dawn. We were kissers, huggers and kidders. Once when Ivrin gave me a lovely card I hugged him, 'Now when you see your own mother, you give her a hug.' He laughed kind of sarcastic, 'She'd drop dead of shock.'"

Joel's sister said, "We'd have a crowd over for a shrimp boil. Ivrin hung back and watched. Once when Joel wasn't there, he opened up and joined in. They even competed over family. His allowance was awesome. At the fall semester, he received enough money for the entire year. When he ran short, he'd just telephone home for more."

Without his parents' knowledge, Ivrin bought Joel a new car on his credit and in his name, a sacrifice since he had dubbed his old high-mileage car "The Tractor."

"They fought about the dumbest things," said teammate Sara Pollard. "Once because some girl gave him a flirty look. Joel said a woman could say something to her and it didn't faze her, but if a man said the same thing, she wanted to punch him out."

When he gave her the diamond engagement ring, because of his family's rudeness, Joel refused to wear it in public until Ivrin stood up to them about accepting her. They wondered why he wasted his time and their money on a country tomboy.

Joel's mother ignored the hint dropped by Ivrin's mother when they met, "I like Joel. The last girl Ivrin dated was using him." Her inferences that money could buy anything and no woman could love Ivrin for himself registered with him before Joel.

In order to take her on vacation, he asked his mother for one thousand dollars to take an extra course and she wired the money. Joel asked, "Why can't you just tell them the truth?"

The chinks in his armor couldn't be buffed out. His explanations were good, the apology prizes nice, but she felt penned in by his control. The wining, dining and status of a steady boyfriend lured Joel back. Marriage to a successful man with a profession and the promise of a lavish life silenced her embryo consciousness of why they had chosen each other and what purposes they served.

Teammates found Joel warm and genuine yet some thought of her as a consummate actress and others viewed her as a gifted con artist. An athletic advisor found her diamonds-or-dirt existence disturbing. She had style in putting clothes together but one lean semester wore the same frayed loafers. The advisor approached the subject delicately, "Are you getting any help from home?"

"It's sort of off and on. My mother can't manage money and when she blows it, we have to gear down."

"The rules prohibit giving you money outright. Babysit for us and we can help with what you need. Let's start with a new pair of shoes." She beamed her million-dollar smile.

"Money slipped through Joel's hands, too," said Kim Cameron. "She'd give you her last quarter if you needed it. On a road trip, she skipped eating to buy a souvenir for her little sister. Other times, she returned from Hammond with some expensive gift from her mother."

When Joel's stepfather built their luxurious dream house, Joel's guilt over her mother's sacrifices eased.

Tara Hester, a former teammate from a large family and old friends with poverty, didn't burst any bubbles for benefactors, "Joel's closet was a traffic jam and her champagne taste even in high school earned her the nickname 'Lady Di.'"

.

Chapter 11

Broken Reflections

When Brenda arrived at Northeast Louisiana University, she befriended her new basketball family, gravitated toward Joel Tillis, her wonderful and supportive "big sister" and told her parents, "She's upbeat and generous, always there for me. I've never had a friend like her." Brenda offered Joel much in return: the flattery of adoration Ivrin's duplicities had stripped away.

On the first day of basketball practice, Brenda suffered a severe knee injury that benched her for the season. Physical therapy could not heal the agony of being sidelined.

Joel was an appreciative houseguest at the Spicer home and Brenda praised her, "She's nice, but her boyfriend doesn't like me and is jealous of her friends."

The previous year, NLU had moved toward strict supervision of teammates by housing the female athletes together, an arrangement sound in theory but making consorting more convenient. Loyalties deepened; the players shared everything from shampoo and money to victories and losses.

If one girl had hairspray, they all did and if one had troubles, they all knew about it.

Ivrin came up during weekends and reserved a hotel room for long-winded love making, which Joel endured as she did those mandatory pushups during practices, counting up from one to twenty and beginning again.

Memories of their first two years together seemed eons ago: designer clothes, trips to the Galleria in Dallas or to Underground Atlanta as well as creative surprises on birthdays, holidays and a cruise to the Bahamas. She couldn't recall the ports they'd visited, the name of the cruise ship, the Mambo songs or why they had argued. Too many arguments had passed.

Now that Ivrin was three hundred miles away, Joel considered them technically broken up. After three smothering years, she promised herself never to answer to anyone again. Yet their mind games were entrenched and she found it hard to relinquish her sympathetic posture as a free spirit repressed by jealousy, who entertained others with replays of their seesaw romance. "I'll never go back to asking permission to go to the mall with my friends. We haven't exactly split, are sort of still seeing each other, but he's there and I'm here." Joel had a knack for evasion: "Not exactly, sort of, more or less."

He telephoned frequently and Joel said he attempted to make her jealous, "I've been dating a girl from one of my classes."

"I don't care. Who needs the pain?"

The distance between them during her summer school alone in Monroe made her less pliable to his maneuvers and her old personality resurfaced. Mischief flickered in her eyes, her indolent smile made the gap between her teeth sensual and her movements relaxed to liquid. Space brought perspective. When she second-guessed writing him off, friends said, "Look at who he's friends with; everyone gossips about it. Why do you let him get you down?"

Denial worked equally well for her. Ivrin had explained, "My friend's neat and agreeable. Sure, his gay friends drop by, but he doesn't throw wild parties or blast music. I can't help it if your girlfriends point the finger in another direction."

Medical school compared to a calloused drill sergeant in weeding out the weak. Competing with the regional crème de la crème, Ivrin bumped into the Peter Principle of scholastics. He had reached the level of his competency at Northeast Louisiana University, but his parents' expectations pressed him to the next rung. "Achieve, achieve, achieve," hammered his skull, but his energy and initiative were depleted. Some wondered if he had wanted to flunk medical school. The boy who always did his homework first while neighbor kids rode bikes or skateboards came out to play as a devilish alter ego chanting, "Fail, fail, fail."

The adoration of the preppy blonde who excelled in studies and sports and was generous with her liberal allowance bolstered Joel's self-esteem. In return, Joel gave Brenda acceptance without control and became her support system. Their physical dissimilarities marked—the petite blonde lengthening her strides in gait with the tall brunette four years older—they had everything and nothing in common, but seemed to function as twin minds, spiritual sisters severed at birth and reunited who were social activists resolute in living life their own way.

After her knee injury, Brenda had idle time while Joel stayed busy with campus activities or went home for the weekend. Her need for Joel crossed the line to fixation. Only Joel understood her despair at losing her point guard slot, the physical agonies of rehabilitation and the feeling she had failed her coaches. Caught in their emotional whirlpools, Brenda, Joel and Ivrin were dangerously parallel—competitive, driven to succeed, voracious for attention and in sexual turmoil.

Brenda resented being a pawn in their complex war maneuvers. When she overheard their telephone conversations, they sent her for solitary evening walks along the bayou where she debated her role. Toward the end of October, the season of longing sharpened by waning sunlight, shorter days and another year soon ending, Brenda returned from her walk and found Joel crying and vigorously pressing clothes, her therapy after Ivrin messed with her head. The iron spitting steam burned her hand.

"Why do you even talk to him? Here, let me finish that before you torch yourself." She examined the welt on Joel's hand. Everything unsaid or denied gathered in the charged atmosphere. They still associated with their teammates who understood they were now "best friends." The carillon bells in the school tower could not drown out their conversation and laughter.

They were always together, drank the heady brew of feminist revolution and drew attention—not unwelcome—a kiss-off of hypocritical homophobes and triumph over the male-female struggle for supremacy robbing women of their power.

Older and wiser, Joel kept private matters secret. The darling of her professors, she acted out her public profile of a mentor to Brenda, nothing more. By November, their behavior roused their coaches' bleak recollections of an affair between a former assistant coach and a freshman player, which caused a national sports controversy. They convened behind closed doors; Joel and Brenda caught cold stares and whispers evaporating as they passed.

Davies's intuition hardened to contempt. The smart and bubbly athlete with the flirty grin, expected to be their Great Feminine Hope and an image player to satisfy the administration and the booster club, had betrayed her. When Davies had recruited her, she enthused to her staff, "You'll love Brenda Spicer, makeup and a cute hairstyle, even wears skirts and dresses."

Seething over being faked out, Davies came down on her. "You're not giving me your best in your rehab program." Friends disagreed, "She worked hard, but it was never enough." The subliminal message was quit the team, pack up and go. Brenda must have felt that NLU and the coaches had her on the mat. She wanted no more grief.

In New Orleans, Ivrin was infuriated also. Exiting a laboratory class, he crunched sere magnolia leaves with his sneakers and counted the squares in the sidewalk. *Step on a crack, break your mother's back.* The fraternity sticker on his car window mocked him. Impossible, unthinkable, that he was blowing two courses.

Studying weekends left no time for trips to Monroe pursuing and appeasing Joel, yet he couldn't abide women walking away from him. His self-professed habit was, "Set a goal, make a schedule and stick to my plans."

Joel's contentment without him goaded as she chattered incessantly about Brenda Spicer. Their strong attachment destroyed his concentration and professors at LSU were oblivious to his charm. Observers later said his splintered veneer exposed a person in over his head. Anatomy, equations and medical terms jumbled his mind like hieroglyphics.

Chapter 12
Lady Indians' Infamy

Brenda's murder revived the Lady Indians' infamy of the year before. The Lady Indians were losing their best talent through graduation and their star player's native country wanted her to represent them at the Olympics. After a visit home, officials allegedly barred the player from leaving. Northeast Louisiana University plucked a department head from vacationing and sent him to the player's native country to stand by indefinitely and solicit help from the American Embassy. After weeks of red tape and with the intervention of United States congressmen and senators, the most valuable player deplaned in Monroe to a roll of red carpet, bouquets of chrysanthemums, the university band and roaring fans. Mysteriously, though on scholarship, she drove a brand new car around campus.

Bionic recruitment ran high with extraordinary means used to lure star athletes as replacements. The Lady Indians courted the top talent coming out of high schools and engaged in a tug-of-war with a flagship university much larger, richer and more aggressive.

One coach made things happen. A red-haired beauty with the style of a Rose Bowl Queen, she reigned as NLU's new image-maker. She made frequent trips to Arkansas and suggested to a young prospect, "We need a quiet place to talk away from the pressures." Whisking away the lonely, impoverished girl, the coach piled her with gifts and affection, inspiring her to sign on. The player spoke of soft music, candlelight and long, silky hair bending over her.

The coach lavished her with expensive electronics and invitations to her apartment. The player's open, awkward infatuation and the coach's casual reciprocation unnerved the other coaches as the guileless player swaggered to teammates, "Look, she bought me this whole set of perfume." The presents awed teammates.

An informant from the competing university with inside information lodged a credible complaint with the NCAA. Davies confronted the coach and Davies fired her, but was left holding the bag. The crash reverberated in aftershocks rocking women's basketball as no episode before and a well-publicized NCAA probe shut down the team. They were the first women's college basketball team penalized and placed on official probation for moral improprieties in recruitment. The penalties banned NLU from post-season play, barred Coach Davies from off-campus recruiting and declared the prospect ineligible to play. Even the Regional South Conference where they had held the title for four years barred them from competition.

Homophobia in women's athletics had reached a national level and trickled down as recruiting competition increased and image became as pivotal as winning. In a moral frenzy, schools became more sensitive to the issue of sexuality in sports, for the booster dollars were contributed by the stalwart family values fans. Even heterosexual players felt threatened by the McCarthy-esque atmosphere. When similar rumors surfaced at another college, they hired a male to replace their stunning coach who had left her husband for a female lover.

Davies's confidence eroded as pressures mounted to polish her and her team's profile, "Put on some lipstick. Do something with your hair. Start wearing dresses." The unspoken message seemed to be to ride out the probation, then conjure a miracle by rising to the Final Four again, but do it with feminine pizzazz. The good old boy mentality rankled, but she enlisted friends to choose an expensive new wardrobe. Recapping games on television, she still came across as a tough no-nonsense competitor.

With national viability crippled, morale was low, blame being assessed and shifted and the university edgy. Davies tried containing team romances—but it was like snuffing out blazing oil wells.

Chapter 13

Seeding Gossip

Joel and Brenda attempted to squelch the gossip by defying tradition on several dinner dates with Benjamin Potter and another football player. The foursome drew the desired notice. Booster Club members who hosted athletes for cookouts or overnight stays drew the line at interracial dating. "It doesn't look right for two Lady Indians to be seen with black football players. We should ask Joel to talk to Brenda."

Joel did. "They cheer us at games, slap us on the back and feed us, then put us on a cross town bus. But Heaven forbid dating their sons or daughters and crossing the social line." The double dates were Joel's revenge and ruse, by which she told Ivrin of their fun times as a foursome.

"No sale, babe, I know too much about that guy to be jealous. What you got, he don't want."

On his rare weekends in Monroe, he told Brenda, "Take a hike and give us some privacy" and argued with Joel for letting her tag along.

Joel was apathetic about being alone with Ivrin and said, "I'm not going to hurt her feelings and abandon her. She needs me. She's devastated by being benched. What gives you the right to dictate my friendships?"

Ivrin's difficult courses and the women he deemed devious, causing his failing grades, enraged him. Joel and medical school were trophies earned and he was losing both.

Brenda's mother told her older daughter, "When I called Brenda, she didn't sound right. She seems depressed and upset. But she won't open up."

"I know. She sounds down in her letters, too."

Brenda's mother arranged for time off and drove to Monroe, stopping to buy a bouquet of balloons. The Lady Indians played while Brenda sat on the bench with her bandaged knee. When she saw her mother, she broke into a big smile. Her mother sat in the bleachers with Joel's mother. Exchanging pleasantries, the women chatted about their daughters' closeness—surface talk yet perceptive. According to Joel's mother, "The visit pulled Brenda's socks up. She talked about her mother constantly after that."

Brenda told her parents, "Coach Davies is coming down on Joel and I about our friendship." Her mother voided her contract, worked closer to home and spent more weekends in Jena. In November, the team played in Gulfport and the Spicers attended the game to show solidarity.

Ivrin was also there. During a scramble, an opponent slammed Joel in the stomach and knocked her to the floor, knees drawn to her chest. He laughed and yelled, "Suck it up, Tillis!"

Stunned by his cruelty, Brenda jumped up from the bench and Davies whirled around, "Sit down. Now!" Just the hoopla they needed, her administering TLC in front of a crowd. Brenda retreated to the stands and sat with her parents, who hugged her against their shoulders.

Ivrin's public humiliation was more proof to Joel of the coldness beneath his professed love. The roses he brought had thorns.

"The coaches hauled Brenda and Joel into a series of meetings," said teammate Wendy Ballard. "Brenda would come out crying with her mascara smeared. Joel would storm out dry-eyed and fuming. She couldn't be broken."

Exhausted by everyone pulling them apart, Brenda told Joel, "When you graduate, I'm going wherever you get a job and playing for a new college. I'm not staying here and being a dartboard."

It dawned on Joel, the director of the drama, that the players were writing their own scripts. What began as flattery swelled to a huge mess. Equivocal, she told Ivrin, "I don't know what I want anymore." He couldn't fight the women's proximity to each other.

Before Christmas break, Davies summoned Brenda to her office again. "Over the holidays, you think about what I've said. You're a bright girl; get your act together. You're making life hell on yourself and on all of us with the image you two project. When you come back in January, prepare to follow my rules, make new friends and let Joel do the same."

Brenda also rejected her mother's pleas to stay away from Joel and date nice young men.

Joel invited both Brenda and Ivrin for Christmas break in Hammond. In his annual ritual, Ivrin arrived with gifts for everyone in the household. He was surprised to see Brenda's car and entered the house in a fury as she and Joel prepared to go shopping. Dumping his packages beneath the tree, he glared, "Don't you see enough of Joel in Monroe? Now you butt in on the holidays. Why aren't you with your own family?"

"Why aren't you with yours?"

"This is my family."

Joel's mother consoled Ivrin, "Joel's just going through a stage. She'll come around. You know how she prides herself on being friends with everyone."

Ivrin wasn't buying Joel's load of cow chips about Brenda needing her because of personal problems. When she bought Joel a cashmere sweater and wool slacks, Ivrin yelled, "You try to buy Joel. You don't belong here." The family acted cool toward her and as she packed, Joel apologized.

On Christmas day, while playing sandlot ball with her cousins, Brenda pulled a ligament in her knee again and went to the emergency room. Swelling and pain erased the months of rehab and hopes for the spring season. She phoned Joel with the news of another injury.

"What are we going to do? I'm so lonely and depressed."

"Hang tough. We'll figure something out."

Joel entertained friends with the horror tale of how Ivrin and Brenda ruined the holidays by fighting over her. Her teammates weren't as malleable as her sympathizers at Northeast Louisiana University, "What did you expect? Don't play poor little girl with me. You don't invite a boyfriend you rarely see and a girlfriend at the same time."

"I'm just trying to be there for them." Self-appointed to balance the world, she often whipped up a tempest to lighten the load. When school resumed, Davies called Joel in for a fourth heated session regarding what was viewed as their destructive behavior. Joel objected to being used as a minority poster girl. "Coach, don't accuse someone without proof." She rattled the glass door leaving.

At a laundromat, Joel aligned the seams of her jeans and creased them, a neatness attack giving her away, for as usual, an untied shoelace flapped to the nervous jiggling of her foot. Something was brewing that Brenda did not want to hear.

"They've got us by the throats," Joel said quietly. "We have to cool it for awhile." Brenda gazed through the plate glass window. A couple necked in a parked convertible. Each time the girl reached for the door handle, the boy touched her freckles and buried his mouth in her hair until her hands settled upon his shoulders again as wafting butterflies. How simple love was for them.

"My grades are touch and go," said Joel. "I'm not a quiz whiz like you. My athletic scholarship is used up, so I'm scratching by on student loans. To graduate, I have to focus and get tutoring. I need faculty on my side until I get my diploma. I either pacify Ivrin or he ruins everything; he and Davies might even pull my mother into this."

Ivrin planned Joel's birthday weekend, a brief celebration with others, music and dancing at a club, then hotel reservations. "Brenda isn't invited. This is our time to plan our future." After a token appearance at the party, Brenda returned to the dormitory. Only the fraying hope that she and Joel could soon be together kept her from plunging over the edge.

Before Joel left for the nightclub, she checked on Brenda as she curled in the bed of her darkened room. "Are you okay?"

"No. I'm not okay. I've lost everything important to me," Brenda said.

"My being with him doesn't mean anything. I'm doing what I have to do."

Teammate Wendy Ballard also checked on her, "I'm driving a friend to Bastrop. Get up, wash your face and go with me."

"I can't."

Ivrin, jubilant and in his element, alternately danced with Joel and the teammates he had included. At midnight, they returned to the dorm for Joel's overnight bag. As he waited in the lobby, Ivrin tapped his watch, maddened that she was probably placating Brenda.

Joel argued, "If I don't go, he flips out. If I do, you flip out. I'll see you tomorrow." She instructed Karin, "Watch her. Don't let her out of your sight. Here's the hotel number. Call me only if necessary, okay?"

When Wendy returned, the players gathered around Brenda's bed. "Brenda acts spaced out. We can't do anything with her. She took a bunch of pills. Here's a list she wrote out and she's insisting on driving her car."

Wendy said, "Let's not overreact; this is over-the-counter junk." Wendy rubbed Brenda's cheek and tried calming her, but sluggishly she got out of bed and found her car keys. "I'll be all right."

"I'm not letting you drive."

Ivrin and Joel had barely settled into their room when Karin called, "Let me talk to Joel."

She grabbed the receiver, "What's wrong?"

"Brenda took a bunch of pills. She's loopy, keeps nodding out, but insists on driving her car."

"Okay, keep her on her feet and walk her around. Call Coach Anderson. I'm on my way." Weaving through interstate traffic Ivrin snapped, "I hope whatever she took does the job."

Joel raced up the dormitory stairs and snatched the list of pills, "Okay, Brenda, we're taking you to the hospital." Joel pulled her downstairs as Davies and Anderson drove up. Brenda yelled, "No, I'm not going anywhere with them!"

Davies and Anderson shoved her into the car and Joel and Ivrin followed them to the emergency room. After Brenda's stomach was pumped, Joel sat beside her bed and massaged her hand. Ivrin waited with the coaches and teammates, pacing the floor and staring through the glass doors at the curtained cubicle. As the night evaporated, he kept glancing at his watch and tapping his fingers on the chair's arm.

The doctor wrote, "When admitted, patient's blood pressure was 150 over 100, her pulse 100. By 3:00, blood pressure was lowered to 130 over 90, pulse to 98. Patient is tearful but in good health. Stated she had thought of suicide before. Unable to elicit a particular reason. Has supportive environment, a friend to stay with her. Promised she wouldn't make another attempt."

With so many people in the waiting room, he had reason to believe his patient had a supportive environment. Brenda didn't want her mother to be notified, but they needed the insurance data. Brenda's mother learned she was stabilized, but felt powerless to help her child.

"Any suicide attempt should be taken seriously," the doctor told the coaches. "Normally, we recommend a brief transfer to the Psychiatric Unit." That move might have saved her life. It was promised that counseling would be arranged through the athletic department.

"Okay, if someone stays with her." That had to be Joel—the only person who could keep her quiet. Brenda was whisked away before a psychologist pried the truth out of her. Ivrin peeled rubber back to the motel for three hours of agitated sleep, a weekend shot and nothing settled between him and Joel.

As required, the dormitory assistant had notified university police of the overdose and their report noted, "Coach Davies stated she would take Brenda Spicer to the hospital, come by later and give us the necessary details, but she didn't report back to us. We checked the hospitals and learned Miss Spicer was released in good condition."

Davies turned back the covers of the twin beds in Brenda's room. "Call me if you need me. I'll be back in the morning. I want to take you and Joel to breakfast so we can talk." Brenda overplayed her hand. The worst that could happen had happened. Joel's displeasure showed in the grim set of her jaw.

The next morning, Brenda declined, "Joel, I'm not going anywhere with her. One more rerun of how I've botched everything for everybody and I'll toss my cookies in her lap."

"I'm not going either." She met Ivrin before he left town. More amenable to his rescuing her from the muddle, they agreed to recover their lost weekend on Valentine's Day.

Davies arrived at the dorm and seemed oddly laid-back. "Brenda, you're officially off the team. Joel, you have one month of play left to wrap up four years. For once, I think we're in agreement that this can't continue."

Joel nodded. The shame of facing people inflamed Brenda's cheeks. Staying at NLU was impossible and without Joel and basketball, Brenda had no reason to stay.

Chapter 14

Death Trap

Ivrin didn't believe Joel's reassurances. He wadded his test paper marked with red ink, backhanded a gooseneck lamp and threw a textbook at Joel's picture. He must have been thinking, *Break them*, for what the bitches had done screwing with his head. In his bedroom, plastered with awards and plaques and gold ribbons, he dialed a familiar number in Jena.

"Hello. Hello…is anyone there?"

He breathed hard until she screamed, "Ivrin, stop calling me!" After ignoring Brenda's messages, Joel finally called back, "I thought if I didn't contact you, he might leave you alone. I know him. He's serious this time." She promised they would see things through together.

The Spicer home on a dead-end road without passersby was an ideal death trap. Brenda slept on the living room sofa, in earshot of a car approaching or anyone entering the house and on the coffee table was the pistol her father had bought her for safety driving to and from campus. Monday dawned crisp with the wind herding fog across fields and calming sunlight. She could make it. Approaching spring with tennis and softball weather would dismiss the fall and winter as a bleak interlude. On the lawn, a blue jay dive-bombed a squirrel and the telephone began ringing again at 7:00 A.M. with only exaggerated breathing on the line.

"Leave me alone or I'm going to the police! Joel told me what you said. Try anything and I swear I'll blow you away." Brenda couldn't unplug the phone, because Joel might call. Her bedroom down the hallway, crammed with trophies and stuffed animals, seemed an ambush for being cornered. She couldn't alert her father or her mother without admitting who threatened her and why.

After four more calls in a row with raspy calculated breathing, Brenda wept uncontrollably and called Joel. "He knows I'm alone. I'm afraid he might come here."

"Okay. Settle down and lock the doors. I have classes, but I'll call you this afternoon. We'll think of something."

Brenda tracked her biography in pictures lining the hallway: ancestors and weddings, birthdays, sports championships and school carnivals. A Valentine bouquet of red carnations sent by her father wilted on the dining table. So much had gone wrong in only six months, the exhilaration of signing with the Lady Indians replaced by debilitating fear. At Thursday's conference game, being surrounded by teammates and friends would protect her. Since the hang-up calls continued, Joel came to spend the night. Joel tried reasoning with Ivrin and he insisted, "I haven't called her. She's just grabbing your attention again."

Joel convinced Brenda that involving the Jena sheriff would only stir more trouble. They had to stand up to Ivrin. Joel would call it quits and Brenda would threaten to go to the police. The quandary was, if she broke up with Brenda instead, she might commit suicide and leave her gut-cleansing diary behind.

Joel's recollection, modified over time, was that nothing uncommon happened that night in Jena. Around 2:00 A.M., Brenda's brother, on a spontaneous trip home, knocked loudly and jumped from behind the shrubs to scare his sister.

The next morning, Joel returned to campus. Brenda checked household bills, wrote checks and compiled expenditures. Her father had reminded her, "April 15 is getting close, honey. I need you to help me with income taxes again." Brenda was a math whiz and enjoyed the order of organizing receipts and balancing figures. She packed extra clothes. After Ivrin returned to New Orleans, she could stay on campus until Sunday.

Townspeople saw Brenda driving around the next afternoon as a tourist might. Atop the two-story high school was a green and black sign that read, "Home of the Jena Giants." On the highway, rows of Delta soil trenching the cotton fields as chocolate ribbons reminded her that she hadn't eaten and wasn't hungry. She shivered and considered going back home.

An entrance sign to Harris Hall read, "This is a security zone. Doors are locked between 8:00 P.M. and 7:00 A.M."

Emitting a visible chemistry, she and Joel walked to the café with heads bent in conversation. Then cruising campus, Brenda popped in a cassette of her favorite song. Neither woman sang along as she usually did.

Without a room since resigning, Brenda hugged the right side of the twin bed with Joel scrunched in beside her. Curving in silhouette for ballast, Brenda rolled in a gondola of fevered insomnia. They awoke heavy with worry. An anaemic sun filtered through the single window. Two odd nightstands stacked with books, photographs and dried chrysanthemum corsages, trophies and wall posters of beach umbrellas and Colorado ski slopes crammed into the small space. Brenda felt claustrophobic.

Joel walked to the window to check the weather. The wind scudded the beer cans littering the sidewalk, rattling like bones across stone. Whose bones? In her drama classes and in Shakespeare plays, forbidden love and Oedipus woundings invariably turned to plots of revenge and grave consequences.

That night's Southern States Conference game marked the end of her sports career, a bittersweet finale, leaving Joel more time to study. There would be an opening ceremony of red roses and monogrammed souvenirs for each player, a predicted win followed by nostalgic television interviews, autographing pictures for fans and families with celebrations over cheeseburgers.

Karin considered skipping Thursday classes when the clock radio sputtered rock music. Joel swatted her leg, "No, no, kiddo. Up and at 'em."

"Yes Mama Joel." She had never known anyone like her who had forced her into talking, studying or even socializing. Finally, Karin started conversing so she would leave her alone.

Even before Brenda resigned from college, she had spent more time in their room than in her own. Suite mates Wendy Ballard and Sissy Burke shared the adjoining room connected by a bath with the door left open for conversations. Brenda's normal banter was subdued.

Brenda walked to the cafeteria, a din of clattering dishes and bilingual chatter. It was awkward bumping into friends and teachers, but only her and Joel's emotional reunion and their pact mattered. A girl from English class slid into the booth beside her, "What happened to you? You quit coming to class, then a guy said he heard you were pregnant. Another story was that you'd overdosed. I know you're not into drugs..."

In New Orleans, Ivrin selected his flamboyant ensemble and reviewed his agenda. He had called Joel's mother to coordinate plans for the 600 mile round-trip in the same day. After the game, he would escort her back to the Hammond exit and drive home. "A long weekend with Joel would be great, but I can't stay over. I have to study for a test on Monday."

In truth, tests and classes no longer mattered. The would-be gynecologist and magna cum laude graduate had failed two courses in a pass or fail curriculum. If Louisiana State University didn't yank his slot, he'd have to repeat the full year. After always being first and best, he was desperately hiding the failures from his parents. In January, he had pinpointed the cause of his difficulties. Joel and Brenda throwing him off balance had destroyed his focus, but he would reclaim the woman he loved.

The two women rehearsed the inevitable showdown over lunch. "Sometime this afternoon," said Joel, "I'll lure him to the ice cream parlor. When you show up, he can't go berserk in a public place. He leaves us alone or we report him to the cops." Their agonizing weeks of separation steeled Brenda's resolve.

Joel said, "Hang tough. I'll see you at the dorm after my laboratory class."

Brenda browsed the bookstore for greeting cards. Like children without enough Saturdays or summers, Brenda and Joel celebrated holidays in advance. It was mid-March and they had already exchanged ceramic Easter eggs.

University Police Chief Larry Ellerman, who had once observed the two walking hand-in-hand and acting silly, saw them in front of the station and spoke with them briefly. Brenda drove Joel to shooting practice, let her out at the players' entrance and parked her car. She approached the players' bench, she saw Davies's scowl and warded off conflict, "I'm just here for the game and driving home afterward."

Seeing the tall figure in the bandstand chilled her. On that day, it would all come down. When practice ended, Joel dashed over and hugged Ivrin as always.

Coach Davies later recalled, "I commented to Ivrin how sharp he looked: white slacks and white loafers, yellow shirt with a red and black design and yellow socks."

Wendy hitched a ride back to the dormitory and Brenda said, "Ivrin's here. Joel is breaking it off with him."

"Blow him off," Wendy had often advised. Now she warned, "I know you're tired of advice. But you be careful of him."

Joel's suitemates noticed Brenda's seesaw moods, checking her watch, chatting, laughing too hard and frowning too deeply. They lounged in the room watching *Oprah Winfrey*.

Ivrin reminded Joel, "I want to get your bicycle and ride it to classes." They drove to the mini-warehouse he had rented after graduating. Their mingled possessions pleased him. Joel questioned his housecleaning mania on her busy game day. "Let's just load the bike and go."

He insisted, and she pitched in and helped. Ivrin was rattled and with a final breakup looming, it was practical to get a head start on dividing their goods. Joel removed her ten-speed racer and they selected items to keep or throw away. He tossed away expensive textbooks and her broken director's chair. Ivrin stacked boxes on the left wall of the six-by-nine foot unit and cleared the right side of the concrete slab. The ceiling bulb had burned out so they worked with the door raised for sunlight.

At the dormitory, he unloaded her bike, "Roll it upstairs to your room and I'll get it after the game." Joel wondered distractedly why he didn't just leave it in his car. Her mother was coming to the game and Joel didn't want any scenes.

Joel had a message waiting: Channel 10 Sports wants you at the stadium for a pre-game interview. While Ivrin waited in the lobby, she and Brenda reviewed their strategy. "You stay close to the telephone. After my interview, I'll call to signal we're on our way to the ice cream parlor."

She waited her turn before the cameras and she and Ivrin watched a baseball game. "I want you to meet Jason Santz, the guy Brenda dates." She pointed to a sturdy athlete waving his baseball cap in her direction.

"Brenda's boyfriend, huh? Now, why can't I picture that?" Joel ignored his cat-and-mouse tone. Santz, a likely draft by the New York Yankees, wanted to meet Ivrin, because of his nasty threats upsetting Brenda. He later said it was no coincidence that Joel wanted to introduce them on that particular day, but when he finished batting they were gone.

At the dormitory, Karin found Brenda reading over cards and letters from a file box on Joel's nightstand. She was crying but put them away and pretended nothing was wrong. Sissy Burke remembered, "We talked, watched television, dressed in stages. She used my brush and curling iron. I don't let people use my personal things so we joked about it."

"I hope you don't clean it." Brenda's cryptic remark was interpreted as wanting to leave something behind.

"Around four o'clock," said Sissy, "The first call came in. I'm a curious person, but I didn't ask."

Joel later said that during her interview, she noticed Ivrin walking toward the public telephone. To others she would claim, "He remained with me the entire time."

Karin overheard Brenda say, "'I'm not ready yet. I'm getting dressed.' I asked where she was going."

Brenda laced the truth with a joke. "I'm meeting Mr. Bolden. We have a thing going." Something compelled her to leave tracks.

Sara whooped, "Don't let that lie slip past your lips." Something was up. She would never doll up for him.

At the ice cream parlor, Ivrin and Joel slid into a booth and ordered malts. His expression soured and acid bit his tongue when Brenda approached. *The bitches had set me up,* he probably thought. His face flushed as she eased in beside Joel. "Don't make a scene, Ivrin. You've forced me from college and harassed me. You can't intimidate us anymore or stop us from being friends," Brenda said.

"Shut up! Let Joel talk if she has something to say." Customers stared.

Joel said half-heartedly, "Okay, I will talk. Only a lunatic talks about hurting people. We're fed up with you calling us gay. You've helped create this mess with Coach Davies because of your temper fits in public."

Ivrin and Joel had broken up a dozen times before, but they shared a history, a joint bank account and even had keys to each other's car. After four years of such fusing, Ivrin practically held a mortgage on Joel. His parents, friends and Spicer were temporary interferences. "Until you shoved in between us, Joel and I were engaged. This has nothing to do with my friends. You're both gay, so you think everybody else is."

"This is not about me," Brenda argued. "She broke up with you when you graduated and left for med school, before we became friends." The intense discussion lasted fifteen minutes. The girls thought Joel was still pulling his strings.

He offered to make peace. "I'm just hurt, okay? I need time to adjust. Then I'll bow out. Joel can go her way, I'll go mine and we can all be friends."

Joel accompanied him back to the dormitory to chill any outbursts that might occur in front of her mother. Brenda, sapped by his blistering tirade, sat in her car putting five minutes distance between them before taking the back stairs to Joel's room. Since male visitors in the room were only allowed on weekends, Ivrin waited in the lobby where guests read, watched television or used the phone.

Nervous and guilt ridden in her mother's presence, Joel shoved her fifteen dollars earned at shooting practice into her hands, "Here, no need to let this money go to waste. You'll be in a hurry to leave after the game, so we can eat now at the cafeteria. They have pork chops and red beans."

Ivrin wasn't hungry, "I'll hang here and watch the tube."

Chapter 15
Foreshadowing Signals

Ivrin dialed Joel's room. "Spicer, look, I apologize. Since it's Joel's last game, I bought a surprise gift and need you to slip it in her locker. Can you meet me in front of the Student Union Building?"

Karin overheard Brenda say, "I'll be there."

Minutes later, a second call came in, "I'm on my way."

Brenda didn't sound right and Sara noticed tears, "Where are you going?"

"To one of two places, I guess."

Sara thought she meant going home to Jena or to the game. They planned to sit together and she pressed Brenda, "Where?"

"To meet Ivrin." Brenda's foreboding sounded crazy and Joel would be angry if she discussed it. She chose her words like leaving crumbs to follow. "I—I may not make it back."

"What do you mean you may not make it back?"

"Never mind. It's okay." Sara didn't think much about Brenda going to meet with Ivrin. In February, he asked teammates to hold a Mardi Gras doll for Joel, and in celebration of her birthday, he had them order a cake, flowers and balloons.

Ivrin's hatchback was recognizable so he chose to drive Joel's car. "So where's the gift?" asked Brenda.

"I don't have it with me. It's at my warehouse."

"That's not what you said on the phone." No way was she going with him without talking it over with Joel. "I have to drive Joel to the coliseum first for check-in."

"No problem." Was he thinking it would be best to have Joel stashed at her game anyway? "The gift's a surprise. Don't say anything. Hey sweets, I'm really sorry. Things will be different, I promise."

Why she accompanied the man who had threatened to kill her was a question her parents would ask unceasingly and Wendy would answer simply, "Brenda's spirit was broken. She would have run through a rattlesnake bed for Joel. Presents turned Joel on and Ivrin often enlisted our help with some hokey arrangement. Brenda had to face him down about his threats."

Others said, "Aside from being naive, she was so beaten down she didn't think she had the right to refuse to cooperate with him."

Joel later recalled, "When we returned from eating, Ivrin wasn't in the lobby. Brenda was in my room. I remembered my camera so he could take pictures of my honors ceremony. I gave the camera and five dollars to my mother, 'Ask him to get some film. He wasn't downstairs.' Brenda said, 'Give them to me. I'll be seeing him first.' My mother was in a dither, because I was running late so Brenda drove me. She said, 'Ivrin wants me to go with him to storage to get a surprise gift for you.'"

Joel added, "We cleaned it out this afternoon and I didn't see any gift. It must be small. If it were anything big, I'd have seen it. I'm late. Davies is going to kill me. See you at the game."

Around 5:45, two baseball players walking to the dining hall saw Brenda drive from the coliseum and waved at her. They joined Jason Santz for dinner. "We just saw Brenda on campus."

Brenda still haunted his thoughts. Several friends had warned him of the scuttlebutt early in, but Santz had refused to listen. Then he did listen, gradually perceiving that when Joel fixed him up with Brenda last fall, he had stumbled into something strange. Her mystique was beyond comprehension, but he decided to find her at the game and gauge her wavelength since leaving college. He was disappointed when Brenda didn't show.

The owner of the service station across from the mini warehouses saw a curious scene. At ten minutes before six, a tan car entered the alley. "An extremely tall, dark-skinned man and a young white girl stood there talking. Clean-shaven with close cut hair, he wore a yellow shirt and white pants. The woman was ash blonde, dressed in a plaid shirt and purple slacks. She stood with her hands jammed in her pockets and her head cocked to one side."

That last detail tripped alarm bells for Wendy. She'd seen the Spicer logo often: hands thrust in her pockets and head angled skeptically when she doubted or disagreed. "That's when I knew the girl he saw was Brenda. It told me she had second thoughts about going inside."

The owner spoke with his attendant who closed each evening at 7:00. "Is that an interracial couple over there?" The two men admitted, "It's something you notice in a town this size. They stood outside talking, him at the back of the car and her at the front. Then the man unlocked the door and stepped inside." An incurable nature of being a people watcher, he noticed things and remembered what he saw. He commented to the attendant how the setting sun seemed to plunge into the pine trees.

When the overhead light didn't come on, Brenda heard the rumble of the door being lowered and whirled around. *Later, I visualized that in the shaft of light beneath the door, seeing Ivrin's insane expression, his lips drooling madness as a charging dog, she tried to shove past him.* He slammed both fists on her shoulders. Evidence suggested that Ivrin whipped out a pocketknife and held the blade against her throat, as if to say, *Make a sound and you're dead.* Then, he backed her toward the cleared corner.

Brenda's fingernails, bitten to the quick months ago, were useless. She was being raped again. "I'm begging you. Don't do this!" Police reports indicated that he flashed a knife, he slashed Brenda's bra and her breasts pitched forward.

The station owner glanced through the four-lane traffic. That hunch of something not right chewed on him and he asked the attendant, "What do you suppose they're doing in there for so long?"

Brenda was forced onto the concrete floor, straddled and knees pressed against her shoulders. There would be saliva on her breasts and semen in her nose and mouth. He clamped his hands around her throat—the bones in her neck were crushed.

The service station owner sat sideways in his car studying the metal door lowered almost to the ground. Renters usually left them open to move stuff in or out, especially in good weather. People don't like tight spaces.

In the coliseum dressing room, the time was 6:15, a half-hour since Brenda had dropped Joel off. She always visited the locker room before games. Joel asked Wendy, "Have you seen Brenda?"

"Not since she gave me a ride back to the dormitory after shooting practice. Why?" Joel didn't answer her. Later, the attendant said that as he prepared to close the station, he noticed the couple was still in the warehouse with the door lowered—a dope deal or maybe sex. At 6:30, he glanced again and the car was gone.

After work, Coach Anderson's daughter drove across the bridge to the coliseum and checked her watch—exactly 6:30, enough time to visit her dad and the team in the dressing room before the pre-game ceremony. She saw Ivrin, Joel's mother and her youngest daughter walking to the game. "I almost offered them a ride and then I remembered the NCAA rules. We were trying to recruit Ivrin's sister." The minutes would be crucial and she would remain firm, "The time was 6:30 on the nose."

The band signaled warm-up with drum music and the Lady Indians danced onto the court single file, twirling basketballs in Harlem Globetrotter style, strutting their exaggerated rhythms and tossing light-hearted smiles at spectators. Joel scanned the place where Brenda usually sat.

When Ivrin topped the ramp with her camera, her heart plummeted. As she ran through the center lineup he stood on the sidelines, radiating fury while snapping pictures. She looked unlike a woman collecting laurels.

A fan commented to her husband when Florida State took the lead, "Joel's game is off tonight." As Joel searched the stands again, Ivrin hoisted the camera in the air like a bloody scalp.

Benched or red-shirted players also scanned the crowd and Cynthia "Cync" Crowe asked Karin, "Wonder why she hasn't shown up?"

"She acted funny this afternoon, got a couple of calls that made her weepy and left to meet someone."

Instinctively, the players kept watching Ivrin. Benjamin Potter also watched him. At Mardi Gras, Ivrin had promised him study guides to prepare for his own medical school plans. When he dropped by his New Orleans hotel room on the parade route, Joel was there and tension obvious. "I think my notebooks are in storage in Monroe. When I come for Joel's game, I'll look."

When Joel goofed a play Ivrin yelled, "Air ball! Air ball!" and she gave him a hard look. Paul Bannon found Ivrin's highs and lows sinister. Quiet and easygoing were adjectives most used to describe him. Bannon thought of Ivrin as quiet as a bomb. He watched the cheerleaders doing somersaults, colorful hummingbirds suspended in air. When Ivrin yelled, "Move your ass," Bannon's wife said, "He's bouncing off the rafters tonight."

Kim also noticed Ivrin's frenzied behavior. Since he was alum and NLU was trying to recruit his sister, she made a point of speaking to him. "I could be a window pane," she murmured. "He looked right through me."

"Hey, get with it!" Players, coaches and select fans overheard. Davies, pacing nervously, hands on hips, engaged in a shouting match with a referee, gestured wildly and stomped away. The disaster was overflowing in front of the NLU president, the athletic director, boosters and the press.

An opponent knocked Joel to the floor, the band struck up a spirit song and she jumped to her feet. Ivrin did a hot dog dance, "Way to go!"

Embarrassed, the athletic director explained to his guests, "That's Joel Tillis's boyfriend." He was about to become part of an intricate alibi and would recall, "Ivrin was impossible to miss. He wore a yellow shirt with red diagonals and white slacks."

The killer had a pressing problem—the body in his warehouse needed to be brought back to campus and thrown into the garbage dumpster.

When Benjamin saw Ivrin leave, he worried he might be cutting out before giving him the study guides he had promised. A clock person, Benjamin noticed him leave six minutes before intermission.

Across the bayou, Zachary Gil, a basketball player, left study hall early to see his sister play her last game of the season. On the narrow bridge, Ivrin passed him running in the opposite direction like the devil was chasing him, so close Zachary could have reached out and touched him.

At Harris Hall, Ivrin jumped into his car and sped the 1.9 miles to the warehouse with a change of clothes in the backseat. Wheeling up the alley, Ivrin raised the door and by streetlight lifted the body. Blood trickling from her nose stained his shirt. He wrapped a car rag around her head and he changed clothes.

Rage and sex empowered him with Herculean strength and witty ideas. Brenda felt weightless. Rather than in the hatchback, where other drivers might see her, he propped Brenda in the front seat and strapped her in.

At the science building, lights blazed inside the Wesley Foundation next door but there appeared to be no one outside. Running out of time, he drove Joel's car back to the game. A purse was hidden in his car and there might be bloodstains.

The athletic director spent intermission talking with the graduate assistant in the hall near the main entrance. "Ivrin walked past us on the ramp without speaking. I called out to him. He turned around, stuck out his hand, then the buzzer signaled start up."

Observers thought some saner twin was filling in, "Ivrin had switched moods to meekness and wore totally different clothes." A team manager also observed, "He had changed into tan pants and the jacquard sweater Joel had bought for him at our Northern Lights tournament in Alaska."

Benjamin later said that he thought to himself, *That's weird; his shirt's different. Why would anybody change clothes at intermission?*

Joel and her mother, when asked what Ivrin wore to the game, also described two different shirts, but soon agreed, "He wore the same clothes all day." Joel's mother claimed nothing appeared unusual about her future son-in-law's conduct, nor did she recall him leaving. "He sat right beside me all evening." A dozen or more witnesses would say otherwise.

The conference victory ended a lackluster season. Davies instructed, "Go put your jackets on, mingle with the fans and give autographs."

Kim waited for a team friend and Ivrin was the only other person left on the floor. He'd been wired all evening and to ease the stickiness, she made small talk, "Here we are again, Ivrin. Do you ever get tired of waiting around for Joel?"

Ballooning to hulk, he spewed animosity, "Don't you ever say I get tired of waiting for Joel!"

"What's wrong with you?"

"Nothing's wrong with me. Just don't ever say that again."

He was anxious to say goodbye to Joel and get on the road. The panic she had fought all evening enveloped her and she sneaked covert glimpses at him. Karin broke the silence, "Your last game, Joel, and we won."

"Yep, her last game. I even have a picture of her busting her butt," Ivrin said.

Relieved when he and her family left for New Orleans and Hammond, Joel knocked on dormitory room doors and found the resident assistant who said, "Brenda left a message for me this afternoon that she needed to see me. I looked for her, but she'd gone out." A week before, Brenda had shown her

Ivrin's scathing letter.

Sara Pollard suggested notifying campus police but Joel said, "Let's hold off. We'll find her. We don't need Davies storming in here."

"I wouldn't mind. I've got nothing to hide."

At the campus station, Joel asked a patrol officer to unlock Brenda's car. "I can't find my keys." He forced the door open and she rifled through it. Brenda's gun was in the console. The incriminating death threat letter was gone.

After returning to campus, Kim noticed Joel, Karin Blue and Sara Pollard huddled on the sidewalk. "We're looking for Brenda. Her car's been parked here since the afternoon. We've covered the campus and hangouts. All we can do is wait, I guess."

Joel's melancholy candor in their conversation the week before tramped through Kim's mind, "It's about to get violent and there's nothing I can do."

At 11:30 P.M., Joel drove to Jason Santz's dormitory. "Have you seen Brenda? She wasn't at the game and I can't find her."

"Where's Ivrin?" he snapped. The remark made Joel realize how much Brenda had confided in him. A Sir Lancelot, he posed a threat.

It would be Sunday and Joel's third police interview before she remembered—after Karin gave her statement—that they had driven to the warehouse twice, finding everything as she and Ivrin had left it.

Several players insisted on notifying Davies and the police. "No! Let me do it," said Joel. After all, she and Brenda were best friends. Taking a missing person report, the patrolman noted that earlier when he opened the car thinking it was Joel's, she didn't mention her best friend had vanished. "No, there's no boyfriend in Monroe she could have gone out with." She didn't point them toward Ivrin or the outspoken Jason Santz or tell them how her camera ended up at the ball game.

The desk sergeant roused Coach Davies, "You know how these kids are, probably out with a friend. I'm sure she'll return and drive home to Jena tonight."

Joel was no longer able to leave her family out of it. She called her mother, "Brenda's missing. Did Ivrin follow you home?"

"We just left him at the exit to New Orleans. Why? What do you mean missing?" She promised to keep her mother posted.

She left a message with Ivrin's best friend, "Have Ivrin call me the moment he gets there. It's an emergency." At 1:00 A.M., he returned her call.

Since she was safe by distance, Joel confronted Ivrin in a hysterical state. "Nobody's seen Brenda since she went to meet you. She said you asked her to go with you to storage to get a gift for me."

"I didn't see her. I don't know anything about a gift. I never made plans to meet her anywhere."

"You did see her! You had my camera at the game. I gave it to her along with five dollars for film."

"Oh yeah...at the intersection after I shot pool at the Rec. She flagged me down and gave me the camera. I went to the store to buy film, then to the game and sat with your mother and them."

Liar, she thought, *liar!* Why would he drive a half-block to the gym and fight for a parking space rather than walking if he hadn't planned to leave campus? He hadn't known then he needed to buy film. And why over three miles to a department store when they sold film at the campus   bookstore and nearby convenience stores?

Around 3:00 A.M., a patrolman spotted Joel and four other players and pulled to the curb, "You ladies are out kind of late."

Joel thought it was time to more or less level with him, "We're looking for Brenda Spicer. She's been having personal problems and is despondent." Her brain raced. Maybe Ivrin had shoved her into the bayou to fake her suicide or accidental drowning.

"What kind of personal problems?" the patrolman asked.

"She received a letter recently from a guy which seemed to upset her. I don't know his last name. I've already searched her car for the letter. Her handgun was still there." Before Sara spoke up, Joel thought it best to mention Brenda's supposed meeting with Ivrin.

At the station, he bounced it off other officers. "Whoa! Earlier, Joel Tillis didn't say anything about a gun, a bad letter from someone or Miss Spicer meeting anyone. Ask her to meet us in front of her dorm and clear this up."

Karin, acting as go-between, spoke to the officers outside and funneled the information to Joel who sat in a back corner of the lobby, "It's not bad news, just a couple of questions."

She hesitated going outside and they found her answers outlandish, "In filing the missing person report, why didn't you tell me what you told my partner?"

"It…slipped my mind."

Friends believed that the contents of Brenda's purse, which usually included lip gloss, a wallet with a roll of cash, snapshots of her family and of Joel Tillis, gum and a packet of stickers, were most likely disposed of by Ivrin.

In her dormitory bathroom, Joel emptied Brenda's gym bag of secrets and calmed herself with a glass of wine. The clothes hamper smelled of life, sweat and dried passion. She pried open the clasp of the leather diary with nail scissors and she thumbed through it, *The depression is worse. Ivrin wrote another vicious letter threatening to kill me. I love Joel, but with the heat from all sides, she's wavering and making excuses. Her ambition is stronger than her loyalty.* She read on.

We've visited paradise together and jogged through hell. Now she's running for cover. I've lost my freshman year, my scholarship, my reputation. I'm so scared. I despise being a coward and letting Ivrin run over me.

Friends who knew that Brenda kept a diary believed Joel shredded the damning secrets within its pages and flushed them in the toilet.

Chapter 16

Wild Speculations, Chilling News

Wild speculations surfaced that the university's storage shed was a cheap place for sex. Public relations staff assessed damage control and tried to restore calm.

Peculiar as the bizarre hearsay was, so was the odd fever of denial. Two faculty liberals who had held up Ivrin as a role model to motivate their sons deemed it ludicrous that he was a suspect. The chorus in the Northeast Louisiana University's president other ear warned him against taking a risk. Only in tight-knit groups or in phone conversations from home did faculty members and employees voice what they really believed.

Kim Cameron verified the motive to Detective Bill Causey, "The arguments started in November, though Ivrin's jealousy and rages began long before Joel and Brenda met. He hated Brenda and his threats escalated. Joel was caught in the middle and told me, 'It's about to get violent.' Eight days later, Brenda is dead."

Wendy Ballard emerged from her mental fog. Joel hadn't mentioned another male during their talks with police.

Causey interviewed Joel's mother by phone and reflected on why it appeared to him she was protecting Ivrin. Massaging his fatigued eyes, he felt the answer of shielding a child was common. He had seen the phenomenon often—better dead than deviant. Virility was a source of pride that was as fundamental as Bible Belt religion.

Causey bounced the case off District Attorney Scott Taylor. "There's not a lot of evidence, but we're digging up what we can." Taylor tagged Emily Devreaux, his assistant and a rookie, to work with the police. Causey took her to the crime scene around dusk and illustrated the blown light bulb substantiating the service station employees' observation of the partially raised door. To strangle her, Ivrin had to find her throat. With car flood-lights, they searched boxes stacked on the left wall.

Scanning the concrete floor, Crime Scene Technician Jim Gregory saw stains that appeared to be blood. The crime laboratory identified the scrapings as Type A, the same as the victim. Joel, also claiming to be Type A, changed her story and said she remembered cutting her finger there. Once treated at a hospital for a minor injury, the records showed a different blood type from Brenda's.

Picking up garbled signals from reluctant witnesses, the detectives complained, "Northeast Louisiana University needs to decide whether they want this solved or shoveled six-feet under with the victim." Paul Bannon wanted it solved, no matter who got caught in the net. In a private call to Police Chief Willie Buffington, he described Ivrin's behavior at the game switching from wild to mild, "He changed clothes during halftime. He's very clever. You've got to get him before he covers it up."

No one else on faculty was talking and Bannon caught the drift. If the police nosed you out, you answered their questions. Otherwise, hold your breath and hope they don't contact you.

Causey and Peel reviewed their case with the DA's staff, "We know the motive was jealousy. This homicide doesn't fit the outer packaging of a girl emotionally disturbed, because she couldn't play basketball and who had a lot of boyfriends until one of them flipped. Nor was it a three-way deal between Tillis and Bolden and Spicer. Corroborating witnesses are few. It wasn't robbery. She still wore diamond studs and silver loop earrings, two rings, a pendant, a charm bracelet and Joel Tillis's NCAA watch. Friends said her voice could wake the dead if she'd had a chance to scream, so the killer probably threatened her with a weapon or surprised her from behind."

Causey answered the questions circling like pesky mosquitoes and sucking everyone dry: why did she go with Bolden to the warehouse and why did Joel Tillis let her? "He had the power to ruin them by revealing Tillis had kissed him off for a woman."

Jason Santz's coaches called him into a meeting and found no delicate approach, "The autopsy showed Brenda Spicer had either been raped or had sexual intercourse and her rectum was dilated. The police need to know what type of sex the two of you were into."

He whistled through his front teeth. "Stop right there. Nothing. We dated for awhile, but I couldn't lock into her moods so we stayed good friends."

"Did you know she dated other guys, reportedly had sex with them?"

Seventh grade sex education. Bristling, Jason threw out his hand. "Whoa. I'm clean. She hadn't dated anyone regularly. Whoever said she had sex with those guys is making her out to be a nympho to whitewash the truth. Ivrin Bolden terrorized her. The police should ask Joel Tillis who she thinks did it."

Itchy from waiting for Ivrin's arrest, Bannon called Buffington again, "The games are videotaped and kept on file. He was too visible for cameras to miss him. That tape might be valuable in proving he left the stadium and changed clothes." Joel got there first. Days after the murder, she had checked out the tape from the athletic office with the excuse of reviewing her form and returned it damaged.

An informant told detectives about a motel melee during an out-of-town game in Lubbock. "Ivrin cursed Brenda in front of us, said really vicious things to her. His and Joel's fighting shook the walls and he peeled out the next morning with his tires on fire. The next night the team played in Tyler. Coach Davies pulled a room check and found Brenda in Joel's room under the covers in the same bed. She yanked Brenda into the hall and chewed her out."

Investigators contacted Doris Davies again, "We're checking on a story that you caught Spicer and Tillis in bed together."

"Vicious gossip, there's nothing to it. I didn't feel there was a lesbian relationship."

Kim fed Benjamin Potter's name to detectives. "He knew the minute Brenda's body was found that Ivrin did it and he comes unglued when we suggest reporting it. He doesn't want trouble, because he's afraid of Ivrin ruining his future career. Talk is Ivrin has a hammerlock on him."

Kim felt guilty and joined Benjamin in the cafeteria, "I had to tell them. They need every scrap of evidence."

He shoved his meal aside, "I don't know anything. So leave me out of it. Don't even bring up my name!"

Causey interviewed him, "We may need you to testify. The DA will contact you." He agreed to cooperate.

Detectives tested the timeframe of the murder with a stopwatch. They arrived at the coliseum at 5:45 P.M., drove to Student Recreation Hall, parked for one minute and proceeded to the warehouse at thirty-five miles per hour. The trip took four minutes and two seconds. They stayed fifteen minutes and arrived back at Harris Hall before 6:15 P.M. "That gave him thirty to thirty-five minutes to kill her and buy the film someplace close by. But he couldn't move the body in daylight. That would have put him walking to the game at 6:30 P.M., when Bryan Anderson's daughter spotted him."

A detective who jogged attended a game to test moving the body. With two minutes left in the half, he took the exit ramp, ran down the coliseum steps and across the bridge to Harris Hall. Climbing into the police unit with Causey and Peel and observing the speed limit, they parked at the warehouse for two minutes. "That's enough time to open the door and retrieve the body." Still doing thirty-five MPH on the return trip, the detectives parked by the dumpster, waited one minute and returned to Harris Hall where Ivrin had switched to Joel's car. Back at the coliseum, the detective raced up the steps, into the hallway and punched the stopwatch: fourteen minutes and forty-two seconds—less than the twenty-minute intermission.

Two weeks after Brenda died, the chilling news telegraphed across campus. Ivrin and Joel were together again—as if they had never been apart.

Chapter 17

Grim Altercation

Strangers asking questions in small town Jena bumped into a colony of silence, so a local resident accompanied Causey. At the Spicer home, a picture of Brenda Spicer's mother as a bride resembled her daughter. In senior portraits, she and her older sister radiated energy and purpose. Her glass unicorn collection caught sunlight through a window. "No, her room is as she left it; nothing's been removed," said Brenda's mother.

Making the rounds, the sheriff told Causey, "Sometimes at night, I'd catch her at the school playing basketball with four or five guys. She trusted everybody and didn't see the dangers."

One of Brenda's coaches wore her blonde hair in a ponytail with trendy clothes. Her closeness to the Lady Indians was a pipeline. She spoke with Causey and scattershot in other directions. She felt Ivrin Bolden could bring them all down like a dam break flooding outward.

Tim Lewis and his wife, who lived near the Spicers, spoke of Brenda's overnight stays at their house. "Yes, she had a diary, was always writing in it. Brenda was bright and funny, popping in for meals and entertaining us with jokes and stories. Something was bothering her, but she wasn't ready to talk about it and you couldn't press her. I cautioned her about close associations with guys having bad reputations and of a married man who flirted with her and wrote a note asking her to run away with him."

The Lady Indians resumed missed classes. Wendy grieved over memories of Brenda acing every course from English to Algebra and controlling the court like a gifted ballerina on stage. They grew up together and shared lazy summers swinging wide on a rope beneath a bridge, plunging arrow straight into the lake, corking to the surface laughing and drying their hair in the sun. Wendy had watched Brenda's fire ground out at Northeast Louisiana University. Her killer only shoveled the dirt on top.

Strutting her jock walk in a T-shirt and cut-off jeans, Wendy saw Sergeant Ed Free parked in his patrol car. "Could I sit and talk with you? I'm upset. People are afraid of ratting on Ivrin and they're turning their backs on Brenda." Free was a pushover for students with problems. Wendy's bravado collapsed and she dove into the curve of his shoulder and cried. "Joel's covering for him. Everybody's zipped up. I feel guilty for not taking him seriously."

"The police and DA are putting it together and he won't outrun it. You couldn't have prevented it."

The towering band of amazon players, trailing specialty in their wake and provoking curiosity, resembled an order of gloomy penitents given to self-flagellation and vows of silence. They agonized over Brenda's acquiescence and hints of mortality as she had gone to her death trap as a sleepwalker. She had faked them off as deftly as court opponents. They saw too late that her hilarity, pranks and toughness changed to passivity.

Justice was police business. Davies's myriad of worries left scant time for those dropping by her office for absolution from fault or venting. Kim tapped on the door pane. Davies brushed her paperwork aside, "So what's on your mind?"

"Why is Ivrin still on the loose? We should have done something to stop him. She was a good person who didn't deserve this to happen to her."

Joel invited Wendy to go for a drive and said in a husky voice, "Fasten your seat belt. I wouldn't want you to get hurt." Wendy's neck stiffened. What was she up to? Joel tuned the radio, and they drove past seedy motels and a sign scrawled in green chalk on a boarded-up café: *Bufet $3.99.* Wendy laughed nervously at the misspelling.

"What's so funny?" Joel snapped. "Can't you see we're caught in the wringer?"

"Where are we going? Look, I'm babysitting tonight."

Joel took a rutted road and parked at an abandoned airstrip. Not a smoker, she retrieved a pack of cigarettes and a flask of wine from her purse. The tobacco haze veiled something unsettled. If Brenda had confirmed their affair to anyone, it would have been to Wendy. Joel gripped Wendy's arm as though squeezing truth from her veins, "What did she tell you about me?"

Terror sped to Wendy's brain. "She didn't tell me anything about you." She and Ivrin were tagging all the bases. Wendy had promised Brenda never to reveal their talks during her low points when Joel had let her take the brunt of things and waffled between her and Ivrin. Wendy's lifestyle at NLU was also hidden from her family, so Joel felt confident of her silence.

Chapter 18

Fear Stalks

Students, assuming a rapist and strangler stalked campus or occupied the next chair in history class, used the escort service. Joel also voiced fear of an unknown killer on the loose. Conversely, she asked suite mates to screen Ivrin's calls. "She told us her exact whereabouts. 'I'm going to the language laboratory. If I'm not back by five o'clock, come look for me.'" Her dramatic aberrations sent foggy messages. If she were afraid, how could she be withholding anything? Not as gullible, police figured blackmail as Ivrin's hold over her.

The squeeze gripped District Attorney Scott Taylor. Their only suspect was far removed from the usual impoverished, uneducated, scruffy defendant. Leaders in the African-American community and sympathizers pressed Taylor. "The cops are railroading him. Their case is flimsier than a nightgown."

A reporter friend told me, "The elements of premeditation and rape, necessary in a first degree murder, seem clear but pose problems. The Biblical role of Pontius Pilate is more prudent: I find no fault with this man. You judge him. A grand jury makes the decision and he's off the hook."

A disenchanted staffer in Taylor's office told me, "We rehashed the case for days. The Boldens had hired Graves Thomas, one of Louisiana's top criminal defense attorneys. The case was a Hollywood event and without a smoking gun, tough to win."

Media wars forced Taylor's hand. A newspaper received a tip that police had searched a warehouse rented by Ivrin Bolden. In a rival leak, television reporters aired it first. Causey told Taylor, "With public suspicion on him, there's a chance he might run."

He agreed, "I guess we have to go with what we have." The whirlwind scramble to convene a grand jury on a few hours' notice mystified reporters and lawyers who settled on two possibilities. Maybe Taylor hoped to convince the grand jury that grounds for a capital offense of kidnapping, armed robbery, aggravated rape and premeditation existed. Though most of those elements were likely, any charges seemed premature. A more thorough probe, coupled with truthful witnesses, might have proven the criteria for first degree. The premeditation and rape were obvious, the victim's bra had been cut with a sharp instrument and her purse was missing.

The state hoped the autopsy would prove rape. Yet the scientific parallel of possible "rough sex" in another trial overshadowed the report. Detective Causey commented, "Yeah, I'd describe strangulation as rough sex."

When Ivrin's name hit the streets, tension divided the community and his attorneys advised him to return to Monroe for an expected indictment. Reporters camped near the courthouse entrances. Inside the jury room with a guard at the door, Joel, subpoenaed as the primary witness, was franker in some areas than she would ever be again. Under Louisiana law, her testimony was secret and couldn't be revealed except by the state in challenging inconsistencies between grand jury and court testimonies. Glaring discrepancies went undisputed.

The indictment took seven hours and Taylor withheld it to allow Ivrin's surrender. A luxury car with gold chrome trim sped into the courthouse basement and while deputies barred photographers, the elevator whisked Ivrin to the fourth floor jail and booked him.

The flood of publicity made a change of venue bid predictable, yet Monroe was the perfect climate for his trial: a university city where image was everything, political power shifting, a first term Taylor running hard and a citizenry putting fairness before race.

Some felt Scott Taylor was a law scholar rather than an aggressive prosecutor.

Some of Taylor's advisors had suggested Devreaux for a proper mix: black defendant, white victim, black prosecutor. The university's vulnerability another concern, an official asked him to contain the sensationalism as much as possible.

Ivrin, rich, brainy and attractive, seemed proof to African-American leaders that black-on-white crime gained more attention and vigorous prosecution. Brenda Spicer was a cadaver in political science.

Seated near Taylor at a banquet, I asked about the rumble over assigning Devreaux, "She's sharp, hardworking, dedicated and involved with the Bolden case from the start. I could have prosecuted it myself, but I didn't think it fair to take it away from her."

It was Devreaux's first criminal prosecution. She had transferred from the New Orleans District Attorney's office. A slim, former athlete, poised and serious in dark suits with curly hair, she shunned fluff.

Chapter 19

A Sinister Hold

Ivrin pled innocent at the arraignment and settled into jail for twenty-five days. His family could've easily posted the $150,000 property bond, but defense attorney Graves Thomas requested a court hearing, ostensibly to ask for bail reduction.

An Irish firebrand feared and revered, Thomas fought hard for his clients. A popular, forty-two-year-old bachelor, he hailed from a prominent line of lawyers and judges, yet the pedigree had never subdued him. Bolting early from his genealogy, he developed gusto for legal combat and a district judge described him as, "A younger, more distilled J. Edgar Hoover—tie loosened, shirt sleeves rolled up and tenacious as a pitbull."

Thomas's stock soared when the Associated Press carried the story of his newest client: "Murder charges brought against medical student."

In "The Hyatt" atop the courthouse, Ivrin had the standard sparse cell with liberal telephone privileges. The jail commander said, "A prominent defendant in a highly publicized case logically needed access to his family and primary attorneys in Shreveport. Better to be accused of favoritism than of civil rights violations."

He learned Joel had retreated to the Camerons to avoid the media and curiosity seekers. Kim found it mind-boggling: in jail yet able to track Joel down. "She's in the guest room studying." Joel hadn't divulged what she had told the stunned grand jury: "Yes, I'm still seeing him. We still plan to marry."

"Kim, don't ever try to keep Joel from me. Now, let me talk to her." He convinced Joel to be his first visitor.

When sleepless nights rolled into troubled dawns, Joel weighed her options: save herself by saving Ivrin or be ruined along with him. By tricking her into helping him clear their warehouse as a deathbed, he could frame her as a co-conspirator.

Joel's dreams were relentless, which included candles flaring in the unlit church of her childhood as she watched her funeral, her frail grandmother fainting and revived by ammonia cap, orange mums in the shape of basketballs being thrown at her casket. Her little sister laughed and ducked her head as she did when Joel teased her. Teachers filed in and lifted her scalp as a cookie jar lid, cramming algebra and history into her skull. Satan rose from the blood-filled Baptismal to claim her body.

Karin shook her shoulder. "Joel, wake up! You had another nightmare." Daylight worse, students she didn't know gaped, "That's Ivrin Bolden's girlfriend. Brenda Spicer's lover." She imagined Detective Causey with an arrest warrant for conspiracy, handcuffing her for all to see. She couldn't prove she hadn't been involved. Ivrin had trapped her as cunningly as he had Brenda and would turn the tables if necessary. Joel envisioned prison, dreary years of inertia and isolation, guarded and regimented, forced lesbianism among the dregs of society—child or husband killers, addicts, psychos—until she also became animalistic.

It was rumored that from his cell, Ivrin issued specific instructions about where she could go, with whom and her curfew time. Her guard by remote control, he was also said to keep a subtle hold over Joel's mother, narrowing her options as well. Declining a grand jury appearance, Joel's mother accepted Thomas's request to testify as a defense witness at a bond reduction hearing.

Ivrin composed a "visitors list" of people he wanted to see should they come. Ingenious even under pressure, he had thoughtful reasons for including them. Karin, the loyal roommate who adored him, and Joel knew too much. His best friend knew everything. A close friend of Zachary Gil, the state's key witness. Did he think he could persuade or intimidate them to help him or keep quiet? Ivrin's parents waited two weeks to come. Working and arranging legal fees, perhaps from anger and heartache, they gave him time alone in the tank to think.

The Lady Indians, caught up in the thriller, screened the calls from Ivrin's mother. Joel shook her head haughtily in dramatic asides, "I am NOT here. Tell her I've gone to do laundry...that I joined the Peace Corps... whatever."

"Well, tell her I'm thinking about her." Much as Ivrin's mother blamed Joel for the disaster, Joel held the key to free Ivrin or lock him away.

Joel's suite mates complained, "Joel, she knows we're lying but she still calls back."

"What does that lady want? She's never even liked me."

"When Joel discussed the murder at all," said Kim, "She always stopped at the point of factual knowledge, but she said, 'If they find that one letter he wrote to Brenda, he's a dead man.'"

Sara and Cynthia pressed her, "Where are the letters, Joel? And what happened to the bedside shelf where you kept them?"

"I...don't know."

Police often summoned Joel from classes. One teacher, irritated by the disruptions and her moods, advised, "Lay the truth out and be free of it." She alone understood the price of catharsis.

Chapter 20

An Uphill Battle

The pitting of the rookie, Emily Devreaux, against big hitter Graves Thomas became a hot issue. If she won, they would accuse her of persecution rather than prosecution. If she lost, some of the white citizenry would accuse her of pulling punches.

In my office at city hall, the day before the bond reduction hearing, I brought the mayor his afternoon cup of coffee. Before being elected, he was a successful television advertising executive and I had been his copywriter. We shared the same work ethic, the strong bond of doing an important job and making government serve the community. He told me, "I learned a long time ago that you have to treat creative people differently." *He knew I would work fourteen hours straight during a crisis as long as I wasn't penned to clock-watching when things slowed.*

"Mayor, I can't explain it. But I have to take vacation to attend that hearing about the murder case of the ex-co-ed."

The court operated under a judge shop system where lawyers studied the docket and selected one like choosing a flavor at Baskin-Robbins: hard, soft or bland. In hearings, the judge wielded more influence than in criminal trials.

Graves Thomas exposed the state's evidence early with a full year for damage control and creating a lineup of other suspects. Intense media coverage was grounds for a motion to move the trial to friendlier ground.

In a surprise move, Thomas filed subpoenas for forty or fifty key witnesses, including Monroe police officers with their documents and evidence. The phrase "evidentiary hearing" buried in the legalese was a glaring indicator of a sneak attack. Legally, a defendant indicted by a grand jury lost the right to a Preliminary Examination where the court sees the evidence and decides if probable cause existed.

Devreaux filed a motion to quash the subpoenas on grounds the defense could access evidence in the proper order under discovery rules, not under the guise of asking for a bond reduction. In an astonishing move, the judge denied the state's motion and allowed Thomas's pursuit. His unprecedented coup-de-grace surprised prosecutors as he steered the hearing into a three-day mini-trial. The real trial would last only five-and-a-half days.

In a side drama before court convened, Ivrin made faces at friends and relatives and mocked Brenda's supporters with grimaces. Ivrin's mother kept Joel in line. As Causey observed, "Without ever having met her, you could walk into a room of 100 people and pick her out as the one in charge."

Joel, seated beside Kim and her mother, asked for their strength. "I'm not going to look at him when I testify or let him coerce me. I'm going to look at you." Their conversation ended as Ivrin's mother, assuming Kim's notebook meant reporter, shoved in between them and instructed Joel, "Don't talk to her." Kim wanted to note any misinformation from witnesses.

In the ladies' room, Joel asked Kim to hold her new designer handbag. Ivrin's mother burst in and snatched it. "I'll take that." Bolden money had purchased the bag and Kim could forget any bleeding heart influence. Ivrin's message was clear: the purse he had his mother buy and ordered Joel to bring to court was a reminder of what hinged on her testimony.

The judge hit the bench like General Custer: Where had all those witnesses come from? Thomas explained, "We subpoenaed them to appear and to produce the material specified."

"Oh, I didn't read that part of your letter. I'm sure there'll be certain objections. The best probable procedure is to call witnesses one at a time. Ms. Devreaux can object to the particular questions asked."

Later, Devreaux objected to Thomas calling pathologist Dr. George McCormick. "Your Honor, for clarity, this testimony will be used for merits of bond reduction?"

"That's correct. That's what we're here for."

McCormick was a scientist who didn't deal in conjecture, though creative prosecutors could transform his findings to advantage by phrasing their questions well. "Yes, the deceased had recently had sexual intercourse with sperm present in the vagina and the rectum. We photographed vaginal fluids that ran down the leg by gravity towards the hip—possibly some of the secretions ran into the rectum. The rectum was dilated, suggestive of but not conclusive of rectal intercourse."

"Any tissue damage or anything similar?"

Devreaux jumped to her feet, "Objection, Your Honor. That's irrelevant to this hearing. The defendant is charged with second-degree murder, not first degree. So any potential rape is not at issue. It's the evidence to indict for second-degree murder that's germane."

Thomas argued, "Your Honor, I'm only trying to establish if intercourse was voluntary or if it occurred in commission of the homicide."

Devreaux was overruled. "Well, I'm going to let him answer the question, but I don't want to dwell too long on it." Her temper soared. Why didn't they just ask each other to dance?

Word spread that Graves Thomas versus the DA's office was a fiery fight. Monroe attorneys cancelled appointments and rushed to the courthouse. District Attorney Scott Taylor never showed up to offer advice or direction.

A red sunset over the river faded to dusk as court recessed for the night.

Ivrin's mother pressed through the crowd, mesmerized Kim with a stony gaze and whispered, "Ivrin wants you here tomorrow in case our attorney calls you to testify." Kim felt she meant the opposite: He didn't want her there and she should think again about her involvement. Joel had to have told him she was scared, knew too much and was close to the cops.

Kim's parents pleaded with Causey, "She'll tell you anything, but please don't ask her to testify."

Chapter 21
Persistence of the Defense

Chief of Detectives Don Hill testified that the defendant had no rap sheet with National Crime Information. Ivrin's problems as a minor inaccessible, Graves Thomas must have felt satisfied they hadn't dug up any secrets.

Detective Bill Causey took the stand and testified about Ivrin. "Yes, I read him his Miranda and he voluntarily gave a statement. No, there was no tape recording of our contacts with him."

Thomas wanted it loud and clear, "THEN HOW DO YOU REMEMBER THE CONTENTS?" A statement based on memory was suspect and could narrow the window of opportunity for the murder.

Piece by piece, Thomas ripped the police investigation apart as irregular and flawed. District Attorney Scott Taylor made his first appearance and expressed his concern to the media that the judge had allowed the bond hearing to turn into a preliminary evidentiary. If the state's case wasn't strong enough, Thomas could ask for dismissal.

The defense would suffer if the service station attendants could identify Ivrin as the man they saw enter his storage unit with a woman the evening of the murder. "Do you recognize him here today?"

"Under the circumstances with him coming in the door with chains and leg irons on, I think anybody would recognize him."

"I mean from prior observation?"

"I believe it was the defendant I saw."

Thomas played the race card, "Did you notice a tall black man who resembled Mr. Bolden and a tall black woman cleaning out that warehouse earlier?"

"No, I only noticed the couple there in late afternoon."

Joel's mother, seated in the corridor, justified her position to several Lady Indians, "I don't see how Ivrin would have had time to do it. I really don't think he did. I've about had a nervous breakdown over this."

In the witness box, Joel's mother laughed nervously, "When we left for the game, a television show was just coming on."

As though expected to sing the theme song, she asked Thomas, "How does that television tune go?" She gave a different time frame than in her original statement, leaving Ivrin unaccounted for twenty-five to thirty minutes. Her claim of sitting beside him all evening differed from other witnesses' testimonies.

Assistant Coach Anderson's daughter, a composed and articulate witness with a resolute memory, had credibility. Thomas wanted her testimony on the table early. She wouldn't be tripped up, even when Ivrin stuck out his tongue at her. "It was exactly 6:30 when I saw him walking to the game with Joel Tillis's mother and several others. I looked at my watch to make sure I was on time and I almost offered them a ride, but it was against NCAA rules. NLU was trying to recruit Ivrin's sister and Coach Anderson is my father."

Thomas deleted her from the defense list. The prosecution added her to theirs; yet shortly before trial the following spring they, too, would drop her. It baffled Northeast Louisiana University personnel that the state rejected her.

The bond hearing, normally taking several hours, was without legal precedent and into its third day. Lawyers agog with news of Thomas picking off cops like ducks in a shooting gallery cancelled appointments and hurried to the courthouse.

Thomas questioned Detective Causey, "Does the police department have a tape recorder to preserve conversations?"

"Yes sir, we do."

"Did you tape record Mr. Bolden's conversation?"

"No, we did not. I wrote a report in reference to it."

"So it's your interpretation of what you heard him say?"

"It's my notes."

Thomas scored again. Fresh out of padlocks at 3:30 A.M., police had left the storage unit unlocked and unguarded. "So anyone might have gone in behind the police, planted the blood spots and tainted the evidence."

"It's possible, I suppose."

"What did you do next?"

"We went to Hammond, searched his vehicle and took a recorded statement from the mother of Joel Tillis."

Thomas echoed, "You didn't record either of Mr. Bolden's statements, the defendant, but you recorded Joel's mother, the witness?"

"Yes."

"You didn't find the victim's purse, nothing indicating Mr. Bolden ever had possession, no sharp instrument on him when you searched him?"

"We didn't search him."

"So you don't really know if he had a sharp instrument or not. Ever find Miss Spicer's journal?"

"No."

"What investigation did you conduct into whether or not he'd been to the department store to buy film?"

"We confiscated register tapes, contacted the sales clerk and showed her a lineup with his picture in it. Register tapes from the camera department showed only two purchases around 6:00 P.M. when the defendant said he was there and paid a little over five dollars for a single roll of 1000 speed film. The first purchase at 5:28 P.M. was for two separate items in camera accessories totaling $6.49. Then at 6:20, two more separate purchases of camera accessories that totaled $7.21. There weren't any single purchases for a little over five dollars."

Detectives who had felt strongly that Ivrin had lied about being at the store when he was meeting the victim hadn't been able to establish where, in fact, he had bought the film. He had tossed them a clue by denying the peculiar point of receiving five dollars from Brenda, presumably afraid they might pinpoint the outlet near campus and a register receipt.

"About the PSE, do you know how that recording came to be destroyed?"

"No, I don't."

Taking the heat for a fellow officer, Causey squirmed about the failure to preserve the tape of Ivrin's PSE question responses—inadmissible anyway. He maintained that erasing PSE answers since you had the graphs was common practice. Nor was it necessarily standard procedure to record statements in a case's early stages. In the usual tactic of trying the police, Thomas suggested ineptitude and intentional destruction of evidence.

Causey appeared wrung out as he left the stand. Implications of a flawed investigation sidetracked pertinent issues and handicapped Devreaux.

Thomas warmed up character witnesses. They vouched that Ivrin was as smart as a Rhodes Scholar, truthful as Opie Griffin, stable as the Brady Bunch. Unready to try the case prematurely, Devreaux hadn't unearthed old skeletons and stipulated to no prior record and his good reputation.

Thomas spoke with reporters, "The state is going with jealousy as a motive. Our client had no motive whatsoever."

The prosecution called the athletic director and a graduate assistant whose gregariousness at the end of the game intermission had interfered with Ivrin slipping back into the coliseum unnoticed. "We stood and talked on an entrance ramp near the exit doors. The second half buzzer sounded as he walked past us."

Zachary Gil, the tall athlete who dated a Lady Indian, testified about Ivrin. "He was running away from the stadium when he passed me on the bridge. Two minutes were left in the first half when I got to the game."

Suddenly, Zachary heard a rumbling noise, "No, no, no." Ivrin's mother, seated on the front row, mouthed, "You're lying. You're lying." A bailiff noted the interference and Zachary, shamed by being called a liar, dropped his head.

"Who was the first person you told that you had seen Ivrin running that night across the bridge?" asked Thomas.

"Peter Marshall, a center on our basketball team."

"What does Peter Marshall look like?"

"He's tall," mumbled Zachary.

Devreaux objected. Thomas argued, "This goes to the motive, bias, interest in the case. Why should the state object to us cross-examining Mr. Gil? We have witnesses to Mr. Bolden's whereabouts conflicting with his testimony. So we're entitled to probe his credibility, his relationship to the deceased, his own whereabouts at the time of the offense."

"Objection sustained."

"Why did you connect Mr. Bolden with this case?"

"The next day people were talking about it and his name kept coming up." Zachary admitted not seeing anyone else he knew going to the game, leaving him no alibi for his own whereabouts.

The agony of Ivrin's mother was palpable. When a witness spoke against Ivrin, she called the person a liar or expressed displeasure. Seeing her suffering, raw dark circles under her eyes, some spectators greatly pitied her.

When Devreaux called Joel to the stand, hers and Ivrin's stories matched as finely as her new purse to her shoes. She said they reduced the bulk of the items during the clean out to a minimum. "One side was covered with boxes, the other with my crates. I didn't see any blood on the floor, cut myself or observe Ivrin cut himself." Although she drew a sketch for the grand jury showing the vacant right corner he had cleared, the state did not produce it or challenge her.

"You spent a lot of time with Brenda Spicer and considered yourself a good friend of hers?"

"Yes, Brenda was a young kid, an incoming freshman. I was a senior and her big sister."

Devreaux changed the subject, "Where do you keep the keys to the mini-storage?"

"In a brown cabinet next to my bed that's unlocked. Other people came in and out of the room, including Brenda." She could have borrowed the keys to rendezvous with any of several tall men.

When the hearing ended, Zachary and his girlfriend walked the seawall across from the courthouse, breathing the river musk and watching the swirling tide. They felt Brenda had become the culprit, along with anyone telling the truth.

The judge issued a statement before denying bond reduction, "The hearings had the atmosphere of a Preliminary Evidentiary. In light of that and based on the evidence presented, there is probable cause the defendant be held for trial."

Thomas roughed him up for the press, "I'm sure the judge is under pressure. It shows he doesn't know the difference between a Preliminary Evidentiary and a Bond Reduction Hearing." Considering the irony, no one disagreed.

"Our purpose was to get the state to show early what it had to build a case. We drew out eighteen pieces of evidence. Much information was disclosed."

Ivrin's father immediately posted the $150,000 bond. Within days, a weekly newspaper released a bombshell announcement: the DA had offered to reduce the bond to $75,000, but Thomas had refused.

In Jena, Brenda Spicer's father found Thomas's victory as disturbing as Ivrin Bolden being free on bail.

Rumors persisted that Ivrin's high school girlfriend had vanished. A Northeast Louisiana University student tipped the DA's office that another girl he had dated escaped his vitriolic courtship with only bruises. Tracked down, she told Devreaux, "He was very jealous, infuriated when I didn't do what he wanted. We argued once and he put his hands around my throat and roughed me up."

According to the DA's chief investigator, "After agreeing to testify, she totally retracted her statement, said she would not do anything to hurt the Bolden family."

After the trial, I asked Devreaux why the woman wasn't issued a subpoena to testify. "We need to know what a witness will say. Otherwise, it could do more harm than good. You don't want any surprises."

Chapter 22

Lightning Strikes

For Graves Thomas, the Ivrin Bolden case was another kingmaker. Four people had died in a boating accident on Lake Bistineau in Shreveport and he had just signed on to represent the driver charged with negligent homicide. Memorial Day weekend, he and his friends partied and water-skied the same lake in his new speedboat. A sudden thunderstorm split the sky, turning the lake dark and choppy. Thomas, reportedly clowning around, stood up in the boat and summoned the lightning, "Here I am! Not even God can make me lose this case."

The next moment a bolt struck him in the head and exited his foot in a blue flash, killing him instantly as his companions who had escaped injury watched in horror. A doctor on a nearby houseboat attempted to revive him while waiting for an ambulance. "We tried everything. It was no use."

The media coverage of Thomas's death, implying he had taunted God and nature on the site where many believed his newest client had carelessly taken three lives, was as flamboyant as his legal career. Even the *National Enquirer* headlined an article, "Zap's Incredible: Boater Fried Alive After He

Dares Lightning to Strike." Friends resented that the playful mental giant died in a squall of sensationalism. When the shock subsided, they realized he probably would have preferred the dramatic ending over a stilted obituary.

The Boldens replaced Thomas with Edwin Greer, another renowned criminal defense attorney.

The Northeast Louisiana University president hoped to calm the wildfire of rumors: "University Tackles the Rumor Mill." He called on staff and employees to "block persistent outrageous rumors pertaining to athletes, coaches, that sort of thing. I can't find proof validating the stories about the Lady Indians or any eyewitnesses. Allegations about team lesbianism evaporate when examined. The team came under scrutiny after the NCAA probation and the recent murder of Brenda Spicer. The advantage of a sports program is its positive impact. If it becomes negative, problems need to be dealt with."

It was said the plan for dealing with the image problem was axing Coach Davies, but not until the hullabaloo passed. Otherwise, it would seem to confirm the gossip.

The statements of the Northeast Louisiana University president exhibited good faith toward the Bolden family, but in a newspaper interview they stated he had visited LSU Medical School and lobbied them to let Ivrin make up his missed classes.

Edwin Greer heard that on the day Brenda died she had talked to the chief of police. Rather than NLU's Chief Larry Ellerman, who had greeted her and Joel briefly that day, Greer phoned City Police Chief Buffington, "I heard you were dating Miss Spicer."

A good-looking family man, he thought he had heard it all during his years in law enforcement. He lifted weights, dressed smartly and served on boards. Quick on the draw, he was congenial until someone invaded his turf or shafted him. His back stiffened, "Hey man, I've never even met her."

"Well, I had to ask."

More bizarre was the circulated tale that Brenda's killer had drained her blood. The assistant coroner groaned, "That solves the case. A vampire did it. The police should be looking for a suspect with fangs."

Those not normally superstitious became so. Similar to Graves Thomas's spectacular passing, the girl who had picked thirteen as her basketball number and lucky charm seemed not to rest easy. Kim met me for lunch, "The dorm had emptied for the holidays with a few of us drifting in and out. A former player brought a friend for a visit. They were sitting on the extra bed in Brenda's old room having a loud gay reunion. We heard this crash and they burst into the hallway wide-eyed. Brenda's bed, upright against the wall, had clattered to the floor. They yelled, 'Nobody touched it or went near it! It fell on its own.'"

A reporter in Shreveport told me, "Usually such a case makes headlines here. Coverage was minimal and when I tried to do a follow-up, my station pulled me off it. I sensed heavy politics and an unwillingness to offend prominent black leadership."

The Boldens' solidarity seemed to many a short-lived PR campaign. Ivrin returned to New Orleans to await trial and his parents returned to Shreveport with rare contact; the norm, again.

Greer used the Alfred Hitchcock format, "First establish an alibi and then remove the motive," hardly dreaming so many would abet them. According to investigators, "It appeared as though many witnesses had inside agendas. Keeping those agendas private was more important than convicting a murderer." Some connected to the case were a sexual tree branching outward. A and B couldn't rat on C and D without their own affairs with E or F being exposed.

Former friends avoided Joel and prosecutors noticed a change. "The first few times we talked, she was all smiles and cooperation. Suddenly, *Enemy* was stamped on our foreheads. She realized that to bring it off, she'd better get into character."

Opinions varied as to why Prosecutor Emily Devreaux didn't call important witnesses. Some of her associates said the slanted bond hearing had crippled her will.

Taylor's office administrator had an idea to prove Ivrin had purchased the film near campus. "Why can't we use the markings on the pictures to track the lot of the film to the retailer who received it?" Her suggestion, like many others, ended up on the "things to do list" left undone.

Chapter 23

Web of
Edgy People

Ivrin received an official letter from medical school: "The First Year Promotions committee met, noting your failing grades in five courses. After thorough review, they recommended you be dropped from the rolls. Should you in the future complete a challenging course of study, we could reconsider. With a limited number of positions available, there is no guarantee."

To maintain the defendant's scholarly image, Edwin Greer would push at the trial that Ivrin enrolled in graduate school at Louisiana State University.

Devreaux theorized Ivrin had been in medical school for six months at the time of the murder and already failing; if he had been able to hack it, Brenda might have lived. Soon failing graduate school, Ivrin blamed it on his legal woes.

The long tense summer brought out a new witness. A student told Causey that at five o'clock on March 5, she had waited for her carpool ride on the glassed-in upper floor of the Student Union Building with its aerial view of campus. "News reports kept coming together in my mind. I think I saw Ivrin Bolden with Brenda Spicer the afternoon of the murder." Causey badly needed such a witness. "I noticed a dark male standing near a window. He appeared nervous and impatient like he was waiting on someone. He left and I saw him and a young woman talking on the sidewalk below." Her vague description of him didn't fit. She had waited too long. Her testimony would not stand up in court and would raise the question of why police weren't pursuing the man she described.

In my research, a striking detail of her statement matched. "While he waited, he tapped his fingers on the guard railing." Nervous gestures are akin to fingerprints. Wendy Ballard had spoken of the same habit at times when Joel was with Brenda and ran late. "He drove me berserk drumming his fingers on a chair."

Coach Davies told confidantes of frightening anonymous calls, "The female never identified herself, just dropped slurs and overtones. 'We should get together and have a good time.'"

The web of edgy people anxious for the trial and an end to the deceit expanded. Rumors flew that Ivrin gave Joel orders by long distance. Her curfew time was 9:00 P.M. and only Benjamin Potter could escort her to school functions. The strategy twofold, it would quiet the stir of his and Joel's ongoing relationship. She could lobby Benjamin not to testify for the state and subtly reinforce Ivrin's vindictiveness. He might even expose Benjamin's own private life.

More friends turned away. "Joel was a good person before. It hardened her." Her Lady Di image of charitable character was a tarnished trophy.

Jason Santz looked forward to December: testifying for the prosecution, graduating college and leaving the tragedy behind.He bumped into Joel and asked, "Did you ever find that threatening letter?"

"No, I'm still looking for it."

"Since you were such a good friend to Brenda, I'm sure you'll find it."

From Florida, Jason's mother mailed a new suit for his court appearance. He didn't need it—the trial was postponed. Signing with a major league team, he left for spring training, still expecting to return to Monroe and set the record straight for Brenda. The subpoena didn't reach him, because it was delivered to his old dormitory at Northeast Louisiana University and was marked "No One Home." Finally, someone checked with the registrar and noted on the subpoena "Lives in Florida."

Traveling to Longwood, Florida, I met Santz at 6:00 A.M. on his way to baseball camp. He spoke of the good person he had admired and the mystery of his elimination, "We never understood why I wasn't called."

Another bungle was the subpoena for Brenda Spicer's mother, also marked as undeliverable with the notation, "Works out of town."

When Joel allowed herself to think about it, the rape and the sodomy which authorities believed was necrophilia were impossible to square. Granted jealousy could make someone kill, but to have sex with the dead girl he hated hovered in her mind; but she rationalized the disparity.

Team members noticed Joel seemed to regard her infamy as fame. Basketball became a past laurel and she occupied the spotlight as the indignant fiancée of the falsely accused doctor-to-be. Caught up in the attention, when conscience overtook her, Ivrin corrected it. Even if she dared reverse her statements, it was too late. She had already testified twice on his behalf with the spectre of being charged as an accessory and of perjury.

Ivrin received special permission to videotape Joel's graduation. Critics said, "Indicted and there he was with a camcorder hamming it up. NLU had no choice. He stood accused, not convicted."

He skipped Christmas with Joel's family. Spending it with them would imply that the Boldens were not the close-knit family showcased at trial. Joel's family breathed a sigh of relief. Being around Ivrin now made the Tillis family jittery. Privately, they had advised Joel to dump him after the trial. Ivrin spent the holidays in California with an aunt.

Chapter 24

Friends or Foes?

In January, Joel moved to New Orleans and lived with Ivrin, where he kept watch over her allegiance. If they were still a couple, what motive was there for murder? She worked for a satellite television company and she gave her family breathless accounts of recognition for the most sales.

She told Ivrin, "We need a vacation before the trial." Former basketball player Tara Hester invited them for a weekend in Memphis—unforgettable, because they acted so strange. She had never seen Joel so angry—fuming and ranting about all she had endured with the police, prosecutors and her fair-weather friends. "The bottom line is that Northeast Louisiana University, Davies and the team want me to take the hit so their lives won't be affected. If I told what I knew about the saints dissing me, there wouldn't be a women's athletic program. I'm the devil who ruined Ivrin's life and brilliant future."

Tara Hester later recalled, "It was awkward. Joel discussed Ivrin as though he wasn't there and she was the person about to be tried for murder. He lay on the sofa and didn't say anything. Finally I asked, 'Well, Ivrin, what do you think about all this?'"

"She doesn't understand what I've gone through." Tara threw her head back on the chair rest: Heaven forbid. Now they competed over who had suffered the most and who was the victim.

"Joel, if you think the police are out to get you and pin something on Ivrin, aren't you worried? I'd be terrified."

Joel stared into Tara's eyes as she had Brenda's. "Don't ever let them see you sweat. When the lawyers ask a question, you answer yes or no, but you don't volunteer anything."

The next morning Tara found Joel and Ivrin in the kitchen rehearsing their court testimony like one of Joel's college plays.

Chapter 25

The Eleventh Hour

The major murder case was reset twice. Yet days before trial, Emily Devreaux and co-counsel Jack Eberlee pared their witness list from fifty to thirty-eight. Rumors flew they had eliminated vital testimony, didn't have a clear timeline of events and police reports didn't seem reviewed.

In eleventh-hour preparations, Devreaux interviewed the Lady Indians she would call and felt her similar athletic background established affinity.

When Emily Devreaux met with me after the trial she said, "It takes someone they can relate to and trust. I understood the code they live by, so they talked to me. One-by-one, they told me about the sleeping arrangement with Brenda in the bed with Joel or on the floor, about Ivrin's jealousy and threats and described the file box of letters that vanished."

Witness Benjamin Potter cited health problems and a serious medical test. When he skipped out on their appointment, Devreaux tracked him down. Their meeting left him bewildered, "I felt by her questions she hadn't put the puzzle together about how the murder came down. She seemed to know little about what really happened."

Devreaux made a file note to have Ivrin's long distance call records checked as evidence of his harassing calls to Brenda. It was not done and didn't come up in court.

The day before trial, Northeast Louisiana University Police Officers Ed Free and Willie Jones met with Devreaux to review their reports. "We described Joel Tillis's suspicious actions and conflicting statements the night Miss Spicer disappeared. Her panic when a white compact car drove up and she hid in our patrol car. Granted we're not lawyers, but we felt there was a way of eliciting what we knew." They felt Devreaux brushed them off.

Free asked, "Are you or are you not looking at Joel as a suspect or co-conspirator?"

Devreaux's temper flared, "We're looking at everything."

Chapter 26

We the Jury

A second-degree murder conviction meant an automatic life sentence without probation or parole. Greer's challenge was selecting twelve favorable jurors from 150 prospects. Judge James Boddie addressed them, "Jury duty is an inconvenience, similar to being drafted into the Army. Nobody wants to go, but afterwards, you tell stories about it the rest of your life."

He went on, "Only in capital cases capable of imposing the death penalty are twelve of twelve jurors required to reach a verdict. Cases of second-degree murder, such as this one, require only ten of twelve jurors to agree. When we call your name, come forward for voir dire examination."

One juror, her high heels hitting the marble floor like bullets, welcomed her induction. She was winsome and thin with fervent convictions. She had followed the case closely and when summoned as a possible juror, a vision of destiny hit her. "Like a rush," *she told me later*. "I knew I'd be called and picked as jury foreperson. It could be no other way."

She described her knowledge of the case, "I read about it in the newspaper, saw a little on television, but the main sensation was his first lawyer being struck by lightning. I don't know where the dumpster was. I don't have any opinion; I can listen."

"The defense will accept her," said Greer.

"The prosecution also accepts."

Three days later in a side drama, Greer asked Judge Boddie to dismiss her.

Equally engrossing was another juror, a storeowner who was friends with some of the local police. Devreaux asked about his knowledge of the case. "I heard through the grapevine about the basketball team and their coaches being a lot of lesbians."

Judge Boddie's cheeks mushroomed and his eyebrows arched upward. Devreaux and Greer looked startled. "You could have heard a mosquito sneeze," the juror said. "I could see they weren't used to hearing much honesty." Ivrin, cautioned on proper behavior, ducked his head to muffle a laugh. The funniest circus ever and his lawyer expected him to be solemn.

"People come in my shop and talk about different things."

Devreaux's eyes flashed with amusement. "What did you hear that connected those rumors with this case?"

"That some of the girls on the team are lesbians. Another girl involved, some jealousy. It wouldn't affect my decision. All I've heard about the defendant is good."

"I'll accept him."

"So will I," Greer said.

The state sought a balance of white-and-blue collar jurors, tradesmen who hunted and fished, church-going mothers with daughters and grandchildren and a white majority panel. Greer shot down the college degrees and the duck hunters. He needed a couple of strong leadership personalities and an imbalance of impressionable housewives.

Another juror expected exemption, because of her job at NLU. "I heard the basketball team was involved in drug peddling, that the three of them—Spicer and Bolden and Tillis—were involved in a relationship. But I didn't think there was a lot of evidence when they arrested him."

The state wanted her—her ties to NLU and insight into motive might help. The defense agreed. Spotting the thinness of the case, she hadn't closed her mind to alternate suspects.

The nine women and three men were not a community crossroad. Two were neighbors and friends, another lived in an area of white exodus and worried about retaliation, one had disdain for police and another wanted to free or fry Ivrin and go home.

At the joint swearing-in, Judge Boddie said, "To serve, you must not be physically or mentally impaired or suffer mental problems that might affect your sound judgment."

The judge moved on, "The defendant is presumed innocent and starts with a clean slate. The state's burden is to prove guilt beyond a reasonable doubt." Several jurors didn't grasp the semantics. "Would you need proof beyond a shadow of a doubt, beyond a reasonable doubt as the law requires or beyond all reasonable doubt?"

Ivrin jammed his hands into the pockets of his navy blazer as the hanging party filed out. Ivrin's father was perturbed, but Greer gestured with hands up to explain why he believed white conservatives would free his son.

For months, my head and heart struggled over resigning my lucrative job to research the story and find out the truth about the murder, live on hope and savings or follow a saner path. As always, emotion won. Loyalty to the mayor and commitment to stay the course until he either retired or was defeated ran deep. It was a promise one didn't walk out on before finished.

"I have to do this. I'll stay two more months and find my replacement." His face was a mixture of surprise and hurt as he nodded. Driven to pursue the truth about the murder, my leaving was bittersweet and guilt-ridden.

Chapter 27

For the Prosecution

Spectators jammed the hallway and the courtroom overflowed with reporters, ministers, trial junkies, sports fans, civic leaders and observing lawyers. A disheveled man with long wispy hair, wearing a wrinkled shirt and khakis prowled the aisle and pushed onto a crowded bench. He smelled of wine and urine, but no one vacated their coveted seat. A woman told her companion, "He said he wanted to meet the Spicer family."

Ivrin quipped to the female deputies assigned to the defense table, "I never knew I had so many friends." The women laughed. Ivrin was witty, polished and likeable. The bailiff escorted Tim Lewis in his wheelchair and his wife to the aisle beside the press bench. The somber couple from Jena, close to the victim, were a conversation piece.

Their rancor obvious by their stiff postures, the tall and attractive Bolden family filed in carrying legal pads, the women in designer clothes; a pretty journalism student, clad in jeans and a tight sweater, sat beside them. The journalist, Cherise Gates, and Joel were now best friends. With Joel sequestered until testifying, the journalist took notes and reported to her each evening.

Devreaux filed her intention to use statements by four Lady Indians, Joel and her mother that Brenda had told each of them before she vanished of her plans to meet Bolden.

In her brief opening statement, Devreaux seemed hesitant to some onlookers. "On March 5 the body of Brenda Spicer was found in a trash dumpster where she had been left for dead. Joel spent the night in Brenda's room... uhm...Brenda spent the night in Joel's room, got up and visited just like any other morning, like any other day."

Slowly she went on, "Ivrin Bolden came to Monroe with a plan to kill Brenda Spicer, to get her out of the way so he could have his girlfriend, Joel Tillis, to himself. Why did he do it? He was jealous of their relationship. *Joel* looked at *Brenda* as a *mother*, as a *big sister*, as a friend.

"About 4 P.M., Miss Spicer met the defendant and together they went to the defendant's mini warehouse."

Causey, seated at the prosecutor's table, suppressed his alarm and twisted his wedding band. He felt Devreaux wasn't expressing the sequence fully and that would blow the foundation of their case.

"Ivrin had a plan for Brenda Spicer. He executed his plan, confronted her and strangled her, raped her and left her for dead in his mini warehouse. Now he's very intelligent, a college graduate. He had to establish his alibi and cover his tracks. After he killed her, he went to the ballgame, like it was any other game, any other day. He participated, took pictures and acted normal to create an alibi. But there was a body at his warehouse he had to get out. At halftime, he went there, got Brenda Spicer's body, put it in his car, threw it in a campus dumpster, returned to Harris Hall and ran back to the coliseum to cover himself just like nothing had happened. He talked to his friends, joked around, establishing an alibi. After the game, he returned to New Orleans. He had accomplished what he set out to do, to get his girlfriend back from another girl. The body found in the dumpster was left for trash because he regarded Brenda Spicer as trash."

Over the next four days, Devreaux offered rivalry as a motive then described Joel as sisterly and motherly, Brenda's best friend. Some jurors felt persuaded of mere closeness between them.

Edwin Greer's opener was lean, detailed and emphatic. He pounced on Devreaux, "What the prosecutor just told you is her theory. In fact, she knows much less about this case than you're going to when this trial is over." Greers's just-plain-folks appeal, old as Huey P. Long's tale of being born in a cabin with holes in the floor so big you could throw a cat through 'em, worked. "Ivrin comes from a modest home with parents who worked their way to the top. They taught him to work hard, play by the rules, be law-abiding and life will treat you fairly." Some jurors' homes could fit into the Boldens' garage.

Describing Ivrin and Joel as the ideal couple headed for marriage, he thundered, "We'll show you exactly where Ivrin was when the state claims he was at the warehouse committing a murder. Now he did run into Brenda Spicer. She had dropped Joel Tillis off about 5:46 and Joel had asked her to give Ivrin a camera to take pictures that night."

Greer didn't explain how Joel knew Brenda would accidentally bump into Ivrin on the sprawling campus of 9,000 students before the game and in time for him to buy film. The jury didn't catch it.

"She flagged him down, gave him the camera. He ran to the store and got film. We'll show you that right after six o'clock, Joel's mother, her sister and Ivrin walked to the basketball coliseum.

"We're going to show you pictures Ivrin took at that pre-game exhibition. He was there. He wasn't back at a storage locker committing a murder in a dusty warehouse, removing the body and dumping it without soiling his white pants. See if his clothes were messed up or torn or bloody. The state says he contrived the way he looked so he would have an alibi."

Ivrin's technicolor ensemble had worked better than hunter's orange in deer season to make him noticed, but his flamboyance had also called attention to his switching outfits.

In rebuttal, Devreaux suggested the defendant removed his pants during the rape and murder. She hadn't subpoenaed the team manager who noticed Ivrin wearing tan pants during the second half. Benjamin Potter had also said, "He had on a different style and color shirt." Devreaux didn't question him about it on the stand. Nor would others who had mentioned the change of clothes be called to testify. Joel and her mother's testimony that, "Ivrin wore the same white pants and shirt all evening" stood.

"He had nothing to fear," said Greer. "The next day Brenda Spicer's body was found. He was notified, came back to town and cooperated. The police questioned him. He gave saliva samples and voluntarily let them search his car for hairs and evidence. They focused on a person instead of a general search to determine who might have committed the murder, tried to fit the facts to my client's guilt. After a quick two-week investigation and an indictment, Ivrin was charged."

What he felt was the state's weak case supported Greer's theory of haste to waste his client. Witnesses who had seen Ivrin blow like a sperm whale, though interviewed, weren't subpoenaed. To many, Devreaux and Eberlee seemed unversed in the "specific question technique" to prove their case.

Greer chipped away at the reputation of the nude girl in the blown-up photographs gruesomely displayed in court. His job was to defend his client. "You'll find many curious things about Brenda Spicer. She dropped out of school, tried to commit suicide—a lot we don't know about her, who she knew or dated, spent time with, a lot of loose ends."

Cynthia told Kim, "He's as full of hockey as Minnesota and just as cold."

Greer told the jury, "Your job is to determine whether the state can prove beyond a reasonable doubt that Ivrin is guilty. We acknowledge some tension between him and Miss Spicer—like an older sister going on dates and her little sister always showing up. Some annoyance there, but no reason to kill somebody. The state has a burden of proof. You do Brenda

Spicer no service if you convict an innocent man."

Northeast Louisiana University officers Ed Free and Willie Jones were eager to testify though they bristled from the exchange with Devreaux the day before. After minimal questions Free was excused from the witness stand. Driving to campus in silence, Jones saw teakettle steam rising in his fellow officer. "Spit it out, Ed, I can tell you're upset."

"Yeah, I am. I feel all the prosecution gained from my testimony was that I work for the university. I saw absolutely no venom or desire to prosecute in that courtroom. If the state isn't fired up, how will they convince the jury? I've had lawyers wring me out and hang me up to dry over a D.U.I. case. This is a murder. I felt I was being questioned about a student doing forty in the thirty mile zone."

Chapter 28

Periled Prosecution

Greer questioned coroner Dr. George McCormick, "If she was raped and strangled in a forceful act at the warehouse, wouldn't there be concrete, grit or sand on her buttocks?"

"Not if the force were mental, as being frightened into compliance by threats or a weapon."

Greer pummeled investigators and when Causey testified, Ivrin's mother muttered, "No! That's a lie!" The judge shot her a warning look.

Causey's pride had been stomped at the bond hearing by the defense's accusals of slipshod work. He felt beleaguered. Everything always came back around to Bolden. Surely, the jury would cut through the malarkey.

On cross-examination, Devreaux reacted to Greer's criticisms of the police with a reference to MPD's evidence van as, "the quote unquote Crime Unit."

Causey said, "After Mr. Bolden returned to the police station for questioning, I was told his mother had arrived from Shreveport. He requested to see her. I stopped the interview, told him he was free to go."

"No!" Judge Boddie beckoned Greer to the bench and asked him to stifle the defendant's mother.

Devreaux grilled Causey, "Did you read him his Miranda rights? Threaten, coerce him or offer him any promises or inducements? Does the interview room seal off? Is the door open or closed? At any time, did he request you to stop questioning him? Did you take notes and do a summary of what he said? How can you be so sure it actually reflects what he said?"

She asked Causey to read the Miranda he had recited minutes before. "In the second interview, did you advise him of his rights again? Is that the Miranda you're holding in your hands?"

"Yes ma'am."

"Okay. What rights did you advise him of?"

Causey repeated the Miranda familiar to anyone who had ever watched a television crime show or read a mystery book.

An observing attorney said, "I know of cases lost or tossed on Miranda. I also remember in school padding my essays by rephrasing the same data. It didn't fool my teachers and it didn't fool anybody at that trial. I felt her examination of Detective Causey aided the defense."

To onlookers, a pattern of fancy footwork dominated. The state continuously bounced off the ropes and waited for the bell. Many felt Devreaux had fallen into Greer's trap of claiming everything from violation of civil rights to manipulation of evidence.

"Detective Causey, were your interviews recorded?"

"No ma'am, they were not."

"Is this usual?"

"In just talking to people it's usual."

"Okay. Had Mr. Bolden been advised he was a suspect by the time he gave his second statement?"

"Yes, the night before."

She asked him to repeat the entire contents of Ivrin's second statement based on his notes—an almost verbatim version of the first night's statement Causey had just read. By law, the jury couldn't take notes. If the two readings of the defendant's alleged movements and whereabouts were intended to show Causey had a good memory, took detailed notes and that Ivrin had lied, many felt the state would've failed miserably. The details were laborious. If anything, what the jury probably remembered would favor the defendant.

Court reporter Juwanna Burson noticed something peculiar and told the court administrator, "Normally, jurors keep their emotions and reactions hidden, but one juror acted atypical when Greer cross-examined Detective Causey. She grinned at Ivrin, rocked back and forth and swayed from side to side as though monitoring a tennis game."

Greer painted police detectives as dumb or dense. Causey wondered why Devreaux was holding back many of their reports. In his opinion, the trial was a dog-and-pony show of run out on stage, jump through a hoop, leap onto the pony's back and hang on while he trots in a circle.

One juror rocked from side to side again to the volleys of Greer's adept backhand.

Devreaux abruptly changed the subject by asking Causey, "Now, the area at NLU where the dumpster was, is that in Ouachita Parish?"

"Yes ma'am."

"What about the warehouse, is that in Ouachita Parish?"

"Yes ma'am."

Embarrassed for her, Causey averted his eyes. The parish covered 633 square miles. Wasn't it more relevant the dumpster was the only one between the warehouse and the college?

Once again, she tried a new tactic. "Detective Causey, did you make an investigative report? How long is that report approximately? Show me how thick it is with your hands."

Looking grim, he held his hands about five inches apart. A juror's face wrote the question: Why didn't she just have him bring the blooming files to court?

"So you took voluminous notes. Are you careful when you write rough notes? Are they legible? You can read them?"

He answered "Yes ma'am" to all questions, so much for penmanship. His complexion florid, he returned Greer's derisive stare on redirect.

After lunch, court reporter Burson witnessed another spectacle. As Causey passed the jury box, a juror seemed to be pointing something out and flashed him a grin. She thought she saw him wink as if it was not prudent to snub a juror.

Burson frowned. Was a member of the jury and the lead detective communicating privately? Though uncomfortable with being a snitch, she was required to report such occurrences to the judge. The jurors were held in the deliberation room while Judge Boddie addressed possible bias. He asked Causey, "Could you tell us about that?"

"I don't know anything about it." He couldn't risk an innocent reflex screwing it up.

Chapter 29
Proving
DNA

The state's tottering case depended on DNA: proving the blood in the warehouse was Brenda Spicer's and matching blood, semen and saliva samples to the defendant. Charles Guarrino, the State Police Crime Laboratory technician who had conducted the tests, was a twenty-four-year-old Air Force lieutenant. Though an avid scientist schooled in valid testing versus technical hair splitting, Greer painted him as a careless novice working in an understaffed, archaic facility. His credentials included a medical technology degree from Louisiana State University, on-the-job hospital training, FBI Forensic Serology School and three hours graduate credit in forensic serology. "While working at a hospital blood bank, I typed thousands of samples."

Greer opposed his qualifications as an expert witness and was overruled.

Guarrino testified, "Life Codes does state-of-the-art testing on DNA fingerprinting or genetic typing by matching the DNA of blood cells to a reference sample. The DNA fingerprint is very specific and can determine with 99 percent certainty that sperm cells belong to a certain person. The suspect's blood was Type A and one in every five people has this type. The suspect is also a secretor—80 percent of the population secretes their blood group substance in body fluids, urine, seminal fluid, nasal secretions and saliva. Oral swabs from the victim, nasal swabs and vaginal washings all tested positive for Type A seminal fluid, same as the suspect. Since the victim was Type O, there had to be a Type A donor. Tests of blood stains from the warehouse, on the tissue and car rag found near the dumpster all resulted in the victim's Type O."

Greer's treatment of Guarrino seemed to some onlookers to infer he was a kid with a toy chemistry set and Guarrino fired back. Dissecting Guarrino's work sheets was legal jargon; the seminal results were legitimate. After two hours of debate on rare tests of Glyoxalase and MN, the jurors' faces had the vacant look of beach motels in December.

Court recessed briefly. Causey stood in the foyer by a window studying the logical X formation of walking paths in the nearby park. I asked, "Bill, what do you think?"

"This trial isn't about Brenda Spicer. Nobody cares about her. It's a show for the lawyers."

Rather than back-to-back appearances by opposing serologists for the jury's comparison, two days of miscellaneous witnesses separated Guarrino's testimony from that of Gary Eliot, the defense's paid rebuttal witness from California. "My job title is Senior Forensic Serologist at a non-profit corporation supported by sales to crime laboratories, training of crime personnel and consulting work. We consult with attorneys around the world—from Japan, Germany and Guam—do research and development on crime laboratory equipment and consult for law enforcement agencies outside of California."

His credentials matched Guarrino's—a bachelor's degree in Forensic Science with minors in biology and chemistry. "I trained under a forensic serologist formerly with Scotland Yard for eighteen months. I've testified in more than seventy-five cases."

Greer asked Eliot to assume he'd been consulted to examine blood and saliva samples in a homicide where sexual intercourse was suspected. "In addition to notes and photographs, SERI uses quality control to reduce errors; a double-read technique by another analyst—subject to having another analyst available," Eliot explained.

"Is there a minimum training time desired for a person to do forensic serology and run these tests and sign off on them?"

"At least six months of on-the-job training by a qualified analyst and at least one outside school at SERI or the FBI Academy." Though Lieutenant Guarrino exceeded those qualifications, the point was lost by the two-day gap in testimonies.

"Wouldn't you have examined the suspect's clothing?" Greer asked.

"Yes. I've had cases where the suspect's underwear and trousers were submitted with stains inside and around the fly area. The stains remain there for years unless the clothing is laundered. If the arrest was close to the scene or the time of the crime, I'd have liked to examine clothing in the suspect's house and laundry hamper."

So would we, thought Causey, *if Ivrin hadn't been two hundred miles away and was stupid enough to keep them.*

"What is your opinion as to the adequacy of the testing?"

Eliot outlined, "The data I would need is test procedures or results and the knowns versus analysis scores. It appears the analyst was either very inexperienced or careless in recording and testing."

Devreaux cross-examined, "Mr. Eliot, you've assumed a lot today, haven't you?"

"Yes, any conclusions in a forensic serology case are based on a series of assumptions whether stated or not."

"Did you actually see or analyze any of the substances listed in Lieutenant Guarrino's report? Know how the substances were collected and stored? How long it took Lieutenant Guarrino to analyze them or the types or ages of the machines he used?"

"No, I do not."

"So you're basing your testimony on very little fact?"

"Yes."

"Are you familiar with any of the labs in Louisiana?"

"No, this is the first time I've ever been in Louisiana."

"Now I understand SERI is privately owned. How much money do you receive for coming here to testify?"

"Well, I've been paid a $300 retainer fee; the rest would cover travel time and testimony, evaluation of the report and consulting with the defense attorney. The total bill is $1500."

"$1500?"

"Yes."

Chapter 30

Bird's Eye View

The state called Benjamin Potter. For him, bucking Ivrin would be like tackling the New Orleans Saints single-handed. "I wanted to get into medical school. My reason for attending the game was to see if Ivrin had found some study guides he had promised me."

To prove his bird's eye view of Ivrin at the game, Devreaux questioned Benjamin about coliseum design, goal locations, seating levels, diagonals of his seat in relation to Ivrin's before finally asking, "Was it easy for you to see him?"

"Yes, very easy. About a twenty-degree turn with my head." He pointed to a lady in a pink coat in the courtroom to illustrate the angle and get on with it.

"Did you ever see him get up out of his seat?"

"Yes, a few minutes before halftime. I checked the clock, because during intermission I planned to go talk with him."

"Where did you see him go?"

"Through the exit door. There's a walkway all around the coliseum. I didn't see him leave the outer part of the building. You can't see from the interior if someone leaves the building."

"Did you ever see him come back into the interior?"

"Yeah. In the second half, a few minutes after the game had already started. So I went to his seat and we talked. About ten minutes were left in the last twenty-minute half of the game."

"What did he say when you talked with him?"

"I asked him, 'Hey man, where have you been?' He changed the subject and didn't answer."

Greer cross-examined. "Mr. Potter, do you have a reserved seat at the coliseum?"

"It's not reserved with a sign, but I always sat in the same seat every game. It was automatic."

Greer nodded and smiled, "Do you take a date to the games?"

"No. A friend was with me. Normally, I take, you know, a guy friend."

Next to Zachary Gil, Benjamin's testimony came closest to proving Ivrin's twenty-five minutes or more absence from the ballgame, a fact not lost on him or on Ivrin. Shedding all connections after the trial, Benjamin dropped out of college, legally changed his name and moved.

Chapter 31
Witnesses Speak

The state called Coach Doris Davies to the stand. Co-counselor Jack Eberlee asked, "Coach, did you have a good rapport with Brenda Spicer?"

"I feel like I did." Expressions curdled.

"How would you describe her?"

"When Brenda entered school, she was a very outgoing young lady, enjoyed being around people, joking and laughing, being picked at and came to my office to talk and cut up with the coaches. She got along well with other players, exhibited team spirit and encouraged others to work hard. A good student as far as academics. After her first knee injury, she set a deadline to be back on the floor..."

Eberlee broke in, "Excuse my interruption. Did her demeanor change?"

"During Christmas break, she reinjured her knee. And you know, in January, she acted a little let down, wasn't jovial, sort of worried-looking. She resigned from school on February 10."

"How do you remember that?"

"Well, she came to my office and said...'Coach,' she says..."

Greer rescued Davies with a hearsay objection and Eberlee rephrased, "Okay, did Brenda Spicer develop any particular relationships with any other players in specific? Do you understand what I'm asking?"

"Well, she got along with other players and seemed to have a strong friendship with Joel Tillis."

"Okay, would you tell the jury about the incident involving Brenda and Joel on the road trip in Texas?"

"Well, we went to the mall to allow the team time to roam around and shop. I sat in the atrium area, you know, just watching people pass by. I noticed Joel and Brenda looking in windows. And you know Brenda was hanging onto Joel's arm like a little kid tugging for her mother's attention..."

"...Uh-huh...yes," said Eberlee, "So what was your reasoning for discussing this with them?"

"Well, when we got back to the motel, I told the other coaches about—you know—what I'd observed, said maybe we might need to mention something to them. An assistant coach said he'd seen this same thing. As a staff, we talked to them, because we felt it in their best interest, best for our team and program."

"And that wasn't necessarily about what happened, but what people might have inferred?" The jury tried sorting it out. Davies was worried enough to call a meeting. But she didn't think anything was going on, afraid of what other people might think. The state had opened the gate and then slammed it shut.

"Well, I explained we knew they were only good friends, but others might misinterpret it."

The jury never learned of the foaming fit Ivrin had pitched in the motel lobby during the road game in Beaumont, Texas, or the next night's match in Tyler when Davies had pulled a bed check, found Brenda in Joel's room and ordered her out. Teammates who had heard the yelling in the hallway and had opened their doors to see what was going on weren't asked in court about what they saw.

"After you discussed the mall incident with Brenda Spicer and Joel Tillis, did anything unusual happen?"

"What do you mean?"

"Did you receive any phone calls?"

"I wouldn't say that had anything to do with the incident in Tyler, but the following Sunday morning Ivrin called me. He said, 'Coach Davies,' you know, 'I need your help…to help me get my girlfriend back.' He says, 'I don't get to see Joel very often and it just seems Brenda hangs around and goes with us everywhere.' So I told him I'd spoken with them, was concerned about Joel, because she was just always a super young lady, but recently she didn't listen to us on the floor as she used to. But I thought everything was much better."

Jurors' faces wore question marks about how attentiveness on the court was supposed to help him get his girlfriend back.

"Your team made it to the Final Four team a couple of years ago. Was Joel Tillis a member of that team?"

"Yes."

"Did the team obtain any items commemorating that and could you describe those items?"

"The NCAA gave us watches—a leather dark brown band, gold tone face, with printing inside—NCAA Championship Final Four."

Jurors debated Davies's testimony. "Talk about jammed elevator buttons. We were supposed to remember the victim wore an NCAA watch and regard it as evidence of something funny going on that she said wasn't going on," a juror later said.

Greer cross-examined, "Coach Davies, after Brenda Spicer's second injury, you testified she went into a slump or period of depression?"

"Well…she seemed preoccupied…wasn't as jovial."

"So a number of problems had mounted for her in the spring semester. Then Ivrin called you as an intermediary to help?"

"Well, I wasn't quite certain what Ivrin thought I could do to help him. I felt he wanted to talk to me, because I'd known him and Joel so long and knew Brenda."

"Yeah, because you knew all the people involved. He didn't want to hurt Brenda Spicer's feelings if you could help him solve the problem, did he?"

"I can't speak for Ivrin. I didn't see what I could really do. Joel never spoke of any difficulties with them."

Next, the prosecution called Sara Pollard. Confident after two years of college and basketball triumphs, she no longer stared at the ground as though to shorten her loping height, was engaged and shrugged off labels of women in sports. Nor did she suffer racial hang-ups, for athletics was an equalizer.

Ivrin bugged and crossed his eyes at her as she took the oath. Going against him was tough, but her mother had said, "You got better things to do than memorize lies."

Sara described Brenda as a loyal friend, generally happy in nature, a good student who preferred close friendships over partying.

Over Greer's objections, the judge allowed Sara to describe Brenda's distress and her comments about meeting Ivrin before vanishing.

Devreaux asked, "Sara, I understand that Brenda considered all her friends as second family. Did she do nice things for you?"

"Yes."

"Okay. Did she specifically do nice things for Joel?"

"She bought Joel stuffed animals and some outfits that I know of."

"Describe the outfits for me. Were they cheap?"

"Outback Red bought from The Limited is expensive."

She later told her mother, "I guess I wasn't supposed to say that, because the lawyers argued and the judge called them to the bench. Ivrin stared at me with this, 'Oh yeah? Tell us something else' look."

Sara was excused and realized Miss Devreaux hadn't covered the questions she'd asked her in interviews: Did the two women share the same twin bed? Did you ever see Ivrin angry or jealous or hear him argue with Brenda?

In our interview, Sara said, "It taught us a lot about the court system. You don't get to tell what you know if they don't ask. When Coach Davies and I finished testifying, the team bus had already left for our road game, so I had to ride with her. She talked about her testimony the whole trip—to get the right answers, you have to ask the right questions. The prosecution didn't." She had no clue that the following morning Joel would take the stand and rip her testimony into confetti.

Joel spent two nights in her old dormitory disarming younger players who dreaded going to court. Sara and Wendy shunned her. She entertained those still speaking to her with adventures of living in New Orleans, skirting any mention of the murder.

The guest of two faculty members and their families for two nights, her ambiguous role as a prosecution witness cast her in a nebulous light—conjectures of complicity might've simply been misguided allegiance to the man she loved. Now conscious that she was wasn't the person they'd perceived, they hosted her nonetheless—which she referred to as, "Taking care of me during the ordeal."

Infuriated by the staff that played host, Wendy scoffed, "Joel needs looking after like the Bionic Woman needs chicken soup."

Davies had reminded her players, "We don't know the exact court schedule, so wear dresses to classes each day. No jeans, slacks or casual wear."

They grumbled. "We'll look like clowns. Can't we run to the dormitory and change when we're called?"

"No. You might not have time."

The defense called suite mate Sissy Burke and pressed the false supposition of Ivrin and Brenda making peace. "Miss Burke, there was, at some point, tensions between Miss Spicer and Ivrin Bolden…but not any outright hostility, though? You never saw them arguing, fighting or screaming at each other?"

"No." She hadn't seen the battles, but she knew about them.

"Miss Spicer was known for midnight walks by herself?"

"Uh-huh…whenever she had problems or whatever. And sometimes Joel would go and walk with her, because…"

Greer cut in, "Okay, did you ever go for walks with her?"

He didn't need Joel accompanying Brenda when she was supposedly meeting the Shadow Man who killed her.

"No."

One juror told another, "It's clear to me she was meeting someone. I know the college routine of sneaking out a window for late dates." It didn't occur to her that co-eds now had door keys or entrance codes.

"Miss Burke, when Brenda Spicer said she and Mr. Bolden were having a fling, that kind of fit in with her joking approach to life?"

"I just took it as she was joking because she disliked…"

"…and she may not have really gone to meet him that day?"

"I don't know."

The players walked a tightrope. Four of them were freshmen on scholarships, their ambitions were to play professionally, coach or attend graduate school. Though they lived by the creed of teamwork and loyalty, they needed to stay in good standing with their mentors.

Jurors saw Ivrin flicking his tongue in lizard motions at the Lady Indians in a sexual innuendo. "It bothered us," said one juror, "that he didn't take the trial seriously. We chalked it up to his youth or a defense mechanism."

In the dormitory that evening, the team was oddly hushed and introspective, recalling Brenda giving pointers, helping with their homework, treating them to movies. Memories were slandered by the trial. She too had lived the creed, "All for one and one for all," yet some among their numbers were all for themselves.

The state called the dormitory assistant. "I got to know Joel well; she was honest and would help you out. I also became friends with Brenda. She was fun-loving and happy when she entered NLU."

"Did you see her spend much time with Joel?"

"Yes, I did."

The brief examination ended in another riddle. The dormitory assistant was the only person who'd acknowledged in police interviews actually reading the missing three-page letter threatening Brenda, but she wasn't asked. Devreaux didn't refer to her statement to police: "Two months before she died, Brenda was upset about a letter from Ivrin and asked me to read it. He ordered her to break off the relationship or he would handle it and get Joel back from her. The signature said Ivrin Bolden."

Later, when we talked, I felt the dormitory assistant was also struck by all she wasn't given the chance to say.

When I asked a staffer in the DA's office why, he excused the bungling. "She probably wasn't questioned about the letter because we would have had to prove the handwriting was Bolden's and that the witness recognized it as his." *Had they forgotten the syrupy greeting card letter signed by him that detectives had found in Brenda's car?*

Instead, the next day, Devreaux asked Karin if she had seen the threatening letter. "No. Brenda had read it to me." The secondhand information was struck as hearsay.

Ivrin looked ready to jump the rails when Wendy took the oath. Staring at her in a red shirtwaist dress and pumps, he picked a zit and crossed and uncrossed his legs.

Wendy occasionally stopped by the cemetery and cried at Brenda's grave. She was fearful of making waves until she got her diploma, petrified of Ivrin and of being labeled gay in front of her mother and other spectators.

Appraisingly, Devreaux studied Wendy, "Weren't you and Brenda Spicer suite mates at NLU?"

"Yes. Well, her room, there's a bathroom in between. We had adjoining rooms. She didn't have a roommate."

"Okay. Did you spend a lot of time in her room?"

"Yes. Every time I came in, I'd go over and say hello or she'd come and speak to me. She looked at me as a big sister and always asked advice about basketball."

"Okay, can you describe your friendship with Joel Tillis?"

"I've known her since we played ball together and then we both signed with NLU…a friend."

Devreaux cocked her head, "Oh yeah?"

Ivrin propped his fist beneath his chin and listened closely.

"She was a friend...a teammate...a pal."

"Describe Joel's demeanor the night Brenda Spicer vanished."

"Real nervous and scared. She was worried."

"Did you ever see Joel spending time with Brenda Spicer?"

"All the time. They were best friends. They just…they always hung around together."

Wendy described her perception of the relationship between Brenda and Ivrin. "At the beginning, the three of them seemed to get along well. Then they didn't get along or want to be around each other."

"And that continued until she died?"

"Yes."

Chapter 32

A Mother's Words

For four days, trial goers watched a Picasso-like sketch of the victim emerging. At times, both the prosecution and defense seemed to describe a victim who provoked danger, a neurotic haunted by rape with an insatiable appetite for attention. Appalled supporters talked among themselves. The trial was erasing the effervescent girl with the code of honor who had never been in trouble, was as disciplined as a child of Sparta in sports and studies and shunned wild parties.

The Marquis de Sade pin-ups of her sprawled on a mattress of garbage bags diminished in horror. Depravity coated sensibility in a milky web: a spider tenderly embracing its young with insect lullabies, then belching their frail vertebrae and napping fat beside the feast.

Scattered witnesses from Texas, Florida, Tennessee and beyond who had moved or changed jobs converged in Monroe. The court paid airline fares and most witnesses flew in, testified the next day and flew out. Accommodations at a hotel included meals in the restaurant and room service. Joel's mother spent the week.

Sara had reminded her months before, "At the game, I spent halftime visiting with you. Ivrin wasn't there."

"Oh yes, he was."

Sara asked Joel's mother again during the trial, "Why don't you just tell it straight?"

"I didn't see anything, hear anything, don't know anything. That's what I'm going to say. End of the story, period."

A woman with a sparkling complexion, alert brown eyes and short dark hair, she wore a double-knit top and skirt. Greer described her as an honest and hard-working school teacher and some observers responded to her sympathetically in an instantaneous surge.

Greer asked Joel's mother, "How many occupations do you have?"

"Three."

"Okay. What kind of guy did you find Ivrin to be?"

"He's A-okay in my book. I like him."

"How did you meet Brenda Spicer?"

"I had talked to her on the telephone and she came to Hammond once to visit." Though Brenda had attended all games and usually sat with Joel's mother, she put distance between them.

She described coming to Monroe the day of the murder, "It's a three-and-a-half-hour drive. We left Hammond about 12:30, 1:00 or 12:00, something in that area."

She did remember arriving on campus at exactly 4:00 P.M. and events almost to the minute for the rest of the afternoon and evening. "When we got to Joel's dorm, she wasn't there, so I went on to the store, because I'd forgotten some personal things."

"Okay, what did you buy at the store?"

"Panty hose and a pair of socks." Joel's mother beamed. "That's personal, isn't it?" Some laughed but not everyone found her amusing amid the seriousness of a murder trial.

Nevertheless, several jurors warmed to the comic relief. "When I returned, Joel came in after about ten minutes. Spicer came in about five minutes later."

Major faux pas. Greer corrected her, "That's Brenda Spicer?"

"Yes. Okay. Brenda. I call her Spicer. That's all I knew. I thought it was a nickname until I found out it was her real name." Telling testimony since Joel had switched from Spicer to the more feminine Brenda immediately after the murder.

"Was there anything unusual about her appearance when you first saw her that day?"

"No. Well…Spicer is friendly, you know, a warm sort of person. But this time she acted different. Her face was flushed. I asked her if she was sick. She said no. And I kept feeling her head and said, 'Let me see if you have a fever or something.' I teased her, said, 'You just need some TLC' and she kind of laughed. You know, she didn't act the way she normally acts…"

"Yes, okay," said Greer.

"We walked to the game. My feet were hurting. They took long strides and I was fussing because I'd worn the wrong shoes, so I said, 'Wait a minute now, slow down.'"

"Okay, then did Ivrin go with you to the seats?"

"Yes, we always sat together."

Joel's mother described the pre-game ceremony, "It started at 6:30. I assume it was 6:30. Ivrin was on the floor taking pictures."

"Did he leave his seat at any time?"

"Yes. Maybe two minutes or so before the first half ended. I can't give you an actual time, because I more or less watched the game clock and they set it at twenty minutes and let it count down backwards. He was gone, to the bathroom, I guess, came back maybe six or seven minutes later, maybe five or six minutes." Joel's mother had verified that the half time lasted twenty minutes, rather than the fifteen minutes Greer kept reinforcing.

"During that entire evening and night, was Ivrin acting normal? Not strange or erratic in any way?"

"Not at all. Just laughing and joking, being Ivrin, doing a dance here and there, jo-jacking, you know?"

On cross-examination by Devreaux, she recalled, "Brenda had on a purple belt tied in a cute little knot." *The belt was an interesting footnote buried in my research: not on the itemized list of clothing the victim had worn and unmentioned before. The murderer had to have kept it along with her purse. Maybe it was saved in the habit prevalent among killers to relive the moment.*

"Joel gave me the camera and five dollars for film to give to Ivrin. But Spicer said, 'Give me the camera; I'll see him first.'"

"Did she say where she was going to meet him?"

"I assumed she meant she'd see him downstairs."

"About what time did you leave for the game?"

"I went downstairs at six o'clock or 6:05, but it was...the show... whatever time the television show was just coming on."

"Didn't you originally tell police detectives that you came downstairs about 6:20?"

Joel's mother seemed rattled, "Now you have to give me a chance here. I better straighten that out. I don't get to see much television as far as program times because of my second job. I don't remember telling them that. I may have. I brought in the television show theme song. I'm not really a clock watcher."

"Joel dated Ivrin for four years and brought him home for you to check him out. And you want him for your son-in-law?" Deveraux asked.

"Sure."

"Now Ivrin spent a lot of time at your house; how often would he come to visit when he and Joel were in college at NLU?" The Bolden family listened intently. Only the trial and saving their son bound them to this woman. Her gold-fishing daughter was the reason he was on trial, they most likely thought. Joel's mother was an underling, an encroacher of their son's affection.

"Ivrin came to our house for most holidays."

Devreaux asked, "He didn't go home to Shreveport?"

Joel's mother saw her error—the decorous young man described couldn't tolerate his parents. "Yes...he...you see...both my daughters at NLU came home a lot."

"Weren't his grade reports mailed to your house?"

"Grades? He got some mail there."

"Didn't he actually live in your home at one time?"

"Maybe if I could...I don't know...the summer I guess after his graduation and before medical school. Joel was still in Monroe taking summer classes. So I said fine."

The jurors debated. One said, "I feel Joel's mother put on a show, but hers and Joel's testimonies put the icing on the cake. Ivrin couldn't have committed murder and moved a body if he was with her before and during the game."

Chapter 33

Swelled Outrage

*A*woman in an ankle-length skirt and bow-tie blouse with her gray hair in a donut bun skipped to catch up with me outside the courthouse. The tripping-on-air of her pumps reminded me of tent revivals attended as a child where worshippers danced the aisles in flurries of sawdust. Peering over her glasses with twinkling eyes and a sly smile, she asked, "Honey, all of us have been wondering something. Are you related to Brenda?"

Secondhand lust shoved in her face, she was a voyeur along with trial junkies, soap opera addicts and psychiatrists subsisting on confessions. A writer's clemency is that curiosity is seldom idle, an expedition into the psyche rather than carnal thrill.

"No."

A blush rouged her cheeks. "Well, you just seem so interested by taking notes. We all just thought you might be."

Among the women in the courtroom blessed by childbirth's brush with immortality, the purest love of parent for child, outrage swelled that the victim was being damned.

Eyewitness Zachary Gil also went on trial. His ragged anxiety seemed furtive as he pointed out Ivrin as the man who had passed him on the bridge running away from the coliseum the previous year.

Greer implied the tall black man seen with a young white woman at the warehouse might have been him or his twin brother who had shown a romantic interest in Brenda. "Your girlfriend was a Lady Indian who was benched. And you hadn't planned to meet her until after the game?"

"Right. But I decided to go for the second half because my sister's also a Lady Indian." He planned to find a friend to take him and his girlfriend to her grandmother's house to watch television. With little spending money, being together was enough.

"But you hadn't lined a ride up ahead of time and you didn't have a car? And she didn't have a car?"

"No, we didn't." Greer was making his poverty seem like a crime.

"Your brother tried to date her, didn't he, on a number of occasions? When did their relationship begin?"

"They never went out. They had a class together and were friendly. He called her a couple of times. That was that."

"How tall are you and your brother?"

"We're identical twins. The same height."

"Before today, you only talked to one side, have you not, sir? And didn't we ask to talk to you?"

"Your eyes aren't going to change what you saw. The defense lawyers want to persuade you otherwise. I see no reason to meet with them."

On redirect, Assistant Prosecutor Eberlee reminded jurors that DNA testing showed the assailant as Type A. "Zachary, what blood type are you and your brother?"

"We're O Positive." He didn't glance at Ivrin or his parents. It rankled him that Ivrin's mother had stopped him in the lobby earlier and called him a liar.

She was cautioned against rash conduct, hid in the stairwell and spoke to reporters. Afterward, one journalist commented, "I sympathize, but if I printed what she said about convoluted conspiracies, they'd lock us in the same rubber room."

Northeast Louisiana University in Monroe, Louisiana, was the initial setting of two infamous murders, which resulted in the deaths of two of NLU's most promising stars on the school's NCAA Lady Indians Women's Basketball team, Brenda Spicer and Joel Tillis.

Brenda Spicer was a promising young star on the university's Lady Indians basketball team until her body was discovered.

The body of Brenda Spicer was found in a dumpster on the NLU campus.

The storage unit where Brenda Spicer was murdered.

Brenda Spicer at her sister's wedding.

Joel Tillis poses for the sports pages of the NLU yearbook.

Lady Indians Honors Ceremony as the number two team in the nation. Joel Tillis is the fourth player from the right.

dy Indian Joel Tillis in action on the basketball court.

Joel Tillis and Ivrin Bolden outside the courthouse in Monroe, Louisiana, just after Bolden's acquittal of the murder of Brenda Spicer.

few of the lawmen who helped bring justice to the murders of Brenda Spicer and Joel Tillis (clockwise from top left): New Jersey Detective Scott Fitz-Patrick, Arkansas Chief Deputy Glenn Ramsey, New Jersey Polygraphist Captain Bob Scara, New Jersey Police Detective Ed Perrino, New Jersey Assistant Prosecutor Rocco Minervino, Arkansas Sheriff Dave Parkman, New Jersey Prosecutor Stephen Raymond, New Jersey Detective Michael (Mickey) King.

Northeastern Louisiana University Sports Coliseum, where Joel Tillis and the Lady Indians rose to the Final Four national championship.

Over a year after Joel Tillis's funeral there was still no headstone, only a tin marker labeling the grave where s▮ rests.

Chapter 34

A Lover's Testimony

Two attorneys read the newspaper over coffee at a donut shop and discussed the trial, "Unbelievable. The DA's using Bolden's fiancée as their star witness to help convict him. Why don't they just call his mother?"

Striding purposely to the witness box, Joel wore a pink linen suit with a string of pearls and carried her new designer handbag. Devreaux exchanged amused glances with Eberlee.

One spectator said, "With her boyfriend and girlfriend competing for her, I expected a femme fatale. Instead, this attractive whopper with all the trimmings."

Ivrin must have worried the least and the most about Joel. Nothing shy about her, she behaved as though she was humoring fools. The jurors credited her haughtiness to jabs at her reputation and the unjust indictment of the man she loved.

Devreaux asked, "Was Brenda Spicer your roommate?"

"No, she wasn't."

"Do you know why she resigned from the university?"

"Yes, she was upset and depressed about basketball and Coach Davies calling us in and chewing us out. She said the image we presented wasn't what she wanted, because of previous allegations from the NCAA. She was supposing…that we were…"

"How did you feel about her allegations?"

"She was accusing me of something totally wrong, wanting me to live my life, quote, as society wanted, and I didn't think society should dictate the way Joel Tillis lives her life."

Many onlookers waited for Devreaux to ask: Accusations that you were what? Instead, she ventured, "What about Brenda Spicer's attitude toward Coach Davies's allegations?"

"She was furious. I was a four-year veteran, through after that year, but Brenda was a freshman. Coach Davies said she would pull her scholarship and kick her off the team. So she came down real hard on her, but not on me."

"Okay. Did you tell Ivrin about that conversation?"

"Yes, Ivrin knew what I had…we had talked about it."

He scratched his chin probably thinking, *Careful bitch.*

"When Brenda visited campus after resigning, where would she stay?" Devreaux asked.

"With us in Harris Hall since she didn't have a room. When she was in college, she was always there."

"Okay. Describe your friendship with Brenda."

"My friendship with Brenda? Well, I'd describe my friendship with Brenda as being a big sister. When I was a freshman, an older player, Tara Hester, was my big sister. So I felt it up to me to provide leadership for younger players."

"The afternoon of shooting practice, did she appear any different than usual?"

Joel asked, "Excuse me? Different? Meaning?"

"Attitude wise."

"No, I didn't notice an attitude change."

"Were you upset about her death?"

Joel's eyes were lead pellets piercing Devreaux. "Yes, I was upset about her death! I'd be upset about anyone who was dead."

"Do you know if she kept a diary?"

Joel cocked her head, "A diary, a paper diary? One of those books? Well, she did some writing."

"Okay, has Ivrin ever shown you the emotion of jealousy?"

"Could you explain the emotion of jealousy? Maybe I can help."

"Has he ever been jealous of you?"

"Me? No."

"Did he get along with Brenda Spicer?"

"Ivrin and Brenda respected each other. I mean, it wasn't visible that they didn't get along. They weren't rude in each other's presence."

Devreaux smiled, "It wasn't visible they didn't get along?"

"What I'm saying, they...if Brenda was there, Ivrin was courteous and if Ivrin was there, Brenda was courteous."

"Where are you living at present?" asked Devreaux.

"Since graduation, I've lived some with my mother, also with an auntie in New Orleans."

"Do you also have a mailing address in New Orleans?"

"Yes. I use Ivrin's mailing address." So much for the neutrality of the state's biggie witness. Joel denied living with Ivrin in their New Orleans apartment.

"Are you still dating and engaged?"

"One day in the future we're planning to get married."

Her manner switched to pleasantry as Greer cross-examined. "Yes, Ivrin was a good boyfriend—reliable, respectable, caring and loving. There was a little tension between Ivrin and Brenda. Nothing noticeable. No more serious problem than him wanting to spend time with me."

"Why did Coach Davies feel it necessary to talk to you two?" The strategy was shrewd. Joel and Ivrin were reaping the benefits of Coach Davies's denial that she believed a gay affair existed. By branding Davies homophobic, Brenda's unhappiness could be shifted to her.

This snitch-on-yourself made Joel jittery. "Well, she was making accusations about the image our friendship...the way I took it, implying we were more than just friends because of previous publicity."

"What kind of previous publicity?"

"The team had been on probation and all. So, you know, gossip about the lesbian...lesbian act. She was worried about that...you know...accusing me indirectly of being that. I didn't see any problem with Brenda and me spending time together, so I ignored Coach Davies." Ivrin radiated admiration. Tillis could skydive with an umbrella and land on a mattress.

"So you interpreted it as accusing you and Brenda of a homosexual relationship?"

"Yes, I did, because it wasn't true."

"And how did Brenda react?"

"She was very upset—furious that she couldn't be Brenda Spicer because of someone else dictating her life from a higher level."

Greer said, "Direct your attention to two days before Brenda's death. Tell us about your trip to Jena."

"Brenda was worried about something, alone and scared, and wanted me to come see her. I went to spend the night."

"Was there any unusual disturbance?"

"Well, around 3 A.M., someone banged on the door and it frightened Brenda. When she hit the outside light and opened the door, her brother jumped out at her. He lived out of state and had driven all night. He had scratches on his face from a fight with his girlfriend. Brenda was afraid of him, nervous he had just popped up. The next morning, I had to leave for classes."

Tim Lewis shook his head in disgust. Joel's warped account inferred that Brenda's brother, for whatever ludicrous reason, could have tracked his sister down at NLU, killed her and fled back to Florida—all without being seen. "Did Brenda stay there the next night after you left?"

"No. She came a day early and spent Wednesday night."

Joel had shifted the date she had gone to Jena to Tuesday. In police interviews, she had said Monday. Brenda had spent Tuesday night and part of Wednesday at home with her brother, blowing the fear element. The state missed the discrepancy.

At recess, I asked Eberlee why Bolden's long distance records hadn't been checked to verify the harassing calls to Brenda. He looked surprised and said, "That would have taken a court order."

Devreaux, who was standing nearby, proclaimed, "We...still don't know the relationship between Brenda Spicer and Ivrin Bolden."

"I felt we definitely did."

Greer steered Joel through his lineup of possible villains. "Did Brenda have any boyfriends you're aware of?"

"She'd dated Jason Santz and another guy. I was in her room when Zachary Gil's twin brother called."

"Were you there when she received annoying calls?"

"Yeah, from someone who upset her. She would hang up."

Greer returned to the innuendo that if indeed it was Brenda's blood in the warehouse, she could have pilfered Joel's key and gone there with any one of several lovers or spurned suitors. Joel said her car keys had come up missing, so Brenda and her killer could also have used Joel's car—in case jurors believed the service station attendants' account of a car at the warehouse around 5:50 P.M.

He tackled the speculation that Bolden family money bought and paid for Joel's car. "Why was your car in Ivrin's name?" Ivrin's parents stiffened. They wanted to hear it.

Joel used the gambit learned in public speaking—repeat the question while collecting her thoughts. "Why was my car in his name? Well, I couldn't get one at the time. Since he was a college senior with established credit, he'd get it in his name and I'd pay for it."

Greer attempted to clear up the ticklish reason for Ivrin's photograph in Brenda's car. "Yes, I had a photograph of him in Brenda's glove compartment. We were going to practice one day when I checked my mail and I put it there."

A jury member later said she spotted several bloopers. Why hadn't she cared enough about her fiancé's picture to frame it or stick it on a mirror?

"After Brenda's body was found, did you contact Ivrin and ask him to return to Monroe?"

"Yes, I did. Detective Causey and I were interacting with each other and he asked did I think Ivrin would come back to talk to them. He said he wanted to get a *recorded* statement."

On redirect, Devreaux asked, "You took an oath to tell the truth at a grand jury hearing. Just like you did today?"

"Yes, I did."

"Okay. When you couldn't find Brenda Spicer, you called Ivrin in New Orleans and asked him if he had seen her?"

"I...yes, I asked Ivrin if he'd seen Brenda Spicer that day. The only time was when he got the camera and film from her."

"Do you recall telling the grand jury he denied plans to meet her?" Ivrin leaned forward. This was his first knowledge of Joel's closed-door testimony—other than what she had claimed.

"Yes. What I was saying is Ivrin said the only time he saw her was to get the film for my camera. I said, well, she told me she was meeting you at the Student Union. I mean in front of it. To get a gift for me. He said he didn't know why she said it. He didn't have a gift. That's what I meant by him denying it."

"But you specifically told the grand jury, 'He said he never saw her.'"

Joel floundered nonsensically, "I meant after he received the film. I was talking about after 5:45, whatever time he got the film, but he didn't see her later on." She gripped the arms of the witness chair and cleared her throat. Something about the camera, film and the Student Union unnerved her. Her tongue kept slipping on *film* versus *camera*, *inside* versus *in front of* the SUB.

In my review of the court transcript, Joel had practically said it. The film had been bought from the bookstore inside the Student Union—not at an off-campus store.

"Miss Tillis, how old was Brenda when she died?"

"She was seventeen."

Devreaux corrected her, "She was eighteen. You didn't know your best friend's age?"

In the corridor, urns overflowed with tissues, soda cups and candy wrappers. When a hefty deputy gave Joel an encouraging pat on the back, she flinched. Perhaps they would think she was a liar without integrity or loyalty.

Her lack of emotion troubled the jury, but one argued, "You want to find him guilty because *she* didn't show any remorse? Good God, woman, it's been a year. The average mourning period's about six weeks."

"Speak for yourself. I didn't even know the victim and I feel more sadness than Joel Tillis does."

Chapter 35

Drama on the Stand

Greer called Ivrin Bolden to the stand. His devotion to scholastics, community and God—the dizzied agenda of an Eagle Scout at a Just Say No rally—was intact. "No, I don't drink, smoke, take drugs or use marijuana."

The roster of first and best seemed endless. "In high school I ranked number one as valedictorian, president of Junior Kiwanis, debate team captain, National Honor Society, Teen Community Service Award and Sertoma Civic Trophy. At Northeast Louisiana University, I graduated magna cum laude."

Greer addressed the state's premise that a mother problem lurked in his psyche and asked, "These are things your mother kept in a scrapbook?"

"Yes."

The transcript of failing grades in medical school was also entered into evidence. "Ivrin, as of March 5 of last year, had you received any grades?"

"I don't believe I'd got any grades. I may have taken two tests by then.

I had an exam that next Monday, but due to the situation I was in, I had to miss it. Then I was incarcerated for three and one-half weeks and missed four exams. After being released, I returned to medical school. Knowing I'd have to repeat my freshman year, I stayed the second semester to familiarize myself with the material."

"So you were charged how long after Brenda Spicer's murder?"

"I was charged the following Monday, so I didn't have a chance to return to New Orleans because I was informed there was going to be a grand jury meeting…to stay in Monroe pending indictment. I was released from the medical school roster then entered graduate school." The lies blatant— he was charged and indicted almost three weeks after the murder.

"With this hanging over you, was graduate school difficult?"

"Yes. I found it very difficult to concentrate because my trial date fluctuated. They set it and reset it. So I flip-flopped it with school and it didn't work out very good."

"At this time, do you have an Army commitment?"

"I'm commissioned as a second lieutenant."

Greer slid into the dynamics of the trio and Ivrin's poor English, worsened by anxiety, made it hard to believe he was an honor student. "How did you get along with Brenda Spicer?"

Ivrin used Joel's exact wordage. "There wasn't any conflict. We didn't outwardly display any disputes. We respected each other in each other's presence. It wasn't a serious problem. It's been blown out of proportion. I didn't mind being with the other players now and then. At first, it occurred when Brenda was around, but eventually didn't transpire often. She'd never respect our privacy alone. That grew to uneasiness." His articulation praised by Joel vanished and a transcript would read like another psychological stress evaluation.

"Did Brenda appear to have a lot of problems?"

"At the time, I didn't know of any. That's why we had that misunderstanding. I didn't understand her attachment to Joel. When Joel informed me about her needing support, we reconciled. It helped me understand their closeness. But I wasn't jealous of Brenda, hostile or mad at her. I felt compassion."

"You wrote in a get-well card, 'I'm trying hard to learn to share Joel with someone else.' What did you mean by that?"

"I meant I mostly exclusively had Joel's attention in college and once I had left for New Orleans, we had to learn to be without each other and I had to reposition myself to feel easy with someone else around her more than I was. When I said I hope we can share Joel Tillis, I meant as far as sharing her as a friend."

"All right. What did you mean when you wrote, 'I care about you very much and I am still learning to love you'?"

"Yes, I wanted to...as far as loving Brenda...as I love the other girls on the basketball team."

"You never believed there was a homosexual relationship between her and Joel Tillis?"

"No, not...because Joel Tillis wasn't...the type of life she had led. I knew she wasn't an easy-influenced person."

Recounting the day of the murder, though Ivrin had told the police he hadn't been to his warehouse storage since renting it ten months before, he now claimed, "One of my reasons for coming to Monroe early was to clean it out in the daytime because the light...it had blown out and we had never fixed it." Joel had told police they hadn't known about the blown bulb until they arrived. The state missed the discrepancy.

On cross-examination, Devreaux challenged the logic and logistics of driving to the store to buy camera film. A man in a hurry, she said, wouldn't pass up four or more film outlets and drive six miles round trip in peak traffic hour. The route to the department store had six traffic lights, a stop sign and a low speed zone. The drive, plus parking and making a purchase, given no other customers, would have taken at least twenty minutes.

Devreaux studied him, "How did you learn of Brenda Spicer's death?"

His anger rising, he had a dour expression. "I received a phone call from Joel's mother informing me they had found her dead. I told her to keep me informed as to Joel's, you know, mental attitude. Because she'd be pretty bad off. So that Friday afternoon, I went to her mother's house. If Joel needed just to be consoled, I'd be prepared to return to Monroe. Then Joel called me. The police wanted me to make a *tape-recorded* statement as the last known person who had seen Brenda Spicer."

"When the police asked you to return to Monroe, why did you borrow a car in Hammond instead of driving your own car?"

"I was…I noticed my car smoking. I didn't want to get stuck, broke down. A cousin of Joel's let me borrow his. I told him to check out the problem."

The lengthy question and answer session about mechanical problems, running hot versus cold, proved nothing. Some strongly felt confused as to why Devreaux didn't ask about the police report of Joel's cousin and his girlfriend driving the car all weekend without incident.

A short while later, Greer resumed accusations that the police had zeroed in on his client and looked no further, "Ivrin, what's the first thing the police said to you?"

"They advised me of my rights, I guess…to remain silent. I told them I understood…had no need of a lawyer because I was there to give them information. I didn't ask for a lawyer."

"And who told you that you were a suspect?"

"Detective Peel. After I answered all I knew about this…my events that day. It kind of shocked me. I just expected to give them information and go back to New Orleans. And he asked me, you know, did I kill Brenda Spicer or know anyone with connections to it. He asked me three or four times. I guess to make sure I didn't have any kind of reaction."

"Ivrin, tell the jury. Did you kill Brenda Spicer?"

"No, I did not kill her."

On redirect, Devreaux asked, "The second time Monroe police

interviewed you, wasn't your lawyer with you?"

"Yes, I had a lawyer with me...correct."

"How many lawyers have you had all together?"

"Officially, I...I think three. Our Shreveport attorney consulted with one in Monroe. Graves Thomas was my lawyer also until he died. Richard Goorley was Mr. Thomas's assistant. And Mr. Greer."

"Okay, so that's five lawyers. And you were advised not to talk to the police. You stated you cooperated fully, yet you weren't available after that second interview?"

"Not without my lawyers…no."

"Your relationship with Brenda Spicer has been described as a misunderstanding, a difference of opinion, tensions, uneasiness. How many letters did you write to her?"

"I wrote her one letter."

"Didn't you tell her to stay away from Joel or you'd handle it?"

"Uh-huh (yes)…yes. I did."

"Did that letter improve your friendship with her?"

Visibly angered, Devreaux probably hoped he would blow up in front of the jury. "No...that's why it…went a step further to do a little better."

Reviewing his tough curriculum, Devreaux asked how he could afford time out for weekends in Monroe in January and February yet couldn't stay over the Thursday night after the murder.

"I had a test that Monday I needed to study for."

"Take a look at Exhibit Twenty-nine, a letter from New Orleans dated February 1 advising you of your failing courses. In fact, hadn't you already been told you'd have to repeat your freshman year?"

Antagonistically, he said, "I don't recall. They wait until...until the end of spring semester before any academic judgment. If you failed more than one class, you had to repeat the whole year. So I wanted to learn as much that spring as I can so it would be easier."

"And you sat next to Joel Tillis's mother the whole evening?"

Now too many people knew otherwise. Ivrin contradicted the alibi of Joel's mother. "Well, she was to my left. I was sitting in a row by myself in front of her a row down."

"Wasn't the topic of Coach Davies's meeting with Brenda and Joel about them being lesbians?"

"Now that I don't know. Joel said…she called them in…didn't say why. Just that Coach Davies made them mad."

"Did you suspect Brenda Spicer and Joel of being gay?"

"No, I didn't. I never...suspected anyone of being gay. I knew Joel wasn't...Joel not being was my only concern."

"That's all we have, Your Honor."

The trial wound down with character witnesses. An elderly pastor told of Ivrin's church attendance. "He's a fine boy." A high school teacher testified to his nice conduct. A disabled Sunday school teacher struggled to the stand in a walker to vouch that Ivrin was a Christian. After leaving Shreveport five years before, Ivrin's character witnesses had rarely seen him, if at all.

Chapter 36
Conflicting Opinions

A vocal jury member said, "People beat the drums for him. Why didn't the state have character witnesses for Brenda Spicer?"

Another irritated juror said, "I'll explain it to you real slow. She was supposed to be the victim, not the defendant."

A feisty woman up on current events retrieved her newspaper from her porch. Spotting her neighbor, District Attorney Scott Taylor, wearing a denim jumpsuit and raking leaves, she reprimanded him, "I supported your election, because you promised to clean up the parish. Here you are, cleaning your yard when you ought to be at the courthouse prosecuting that case."

Bailiffs spread the physical evidence on a long mahogany table: Brenda's underwear, shirt and pants. Devreaux wanted the jury to examine them for concrete dust discoloration. The vocal juror, pacing the length of the table as a ponderous sleuth looking for clues, held the severed brassiere in mid-air and studied it.

In the jury's deliberations, the men who hadn't shrunk had grown taller.

Greer had whittled Ivrin's six-foot-six to "about six-foot-one." A jury member, feeling taller under the spell of another, saw height as a reasonable doubt. "The gas station guys said the man they saw at the warehouse was extremely tall. Ivrin Bolden's about my height. The prosecution witness, Zachary Gil, is extremely tall."

A female juror was skeptical about strength. "It's totally unrealistic he could lift 137 pounds of dead weight and throw it into the dumpster. That takes a mighty strong person and a party was going on next door. An intelligent person who got into medical school wouldn't be that dumb."

Another juror argued, "Well, whoever killed her didn't rape and strangle her inside the dumpster then climb back out. I don't care if there was topless dancing with floodlights on the parking lot next door."

Another juror complained to the other. The deliberations wore on. One juror slammed his fist on the table, "You're going for guilty because Joel Tillis didn't show any remorse over Brenda Spicer?"

A resolute juror stayed with guilty and two others badgered him to explain. "It's how he acts that helps convince me. He wouldn't look his lawyer in the eye when he asked if he killed Brenda Spicer. Clowning and making idiotic faces at witnesses, to him a dead woman is no more than a dead rat. We don't have to reach a verdict today. So we're tied up. Let's recess for the weekend, come back Monday with a clear head. We've only been here five days. Other places, trials can last for months." But three jurors driving into the city from rural areas didn't want to run into the next week.

Acrimony and judicial uproar centered on the evidence. After trial, one of the jurors told me, "I really got angry when I asked to see the victim's shirt for the dust and discoloration Ms. Devreaux mentioned. I hadn't noticed any before to suggest she had been on the warehouse floor and I wanted to check. But the bailiff said, 'You've already looked at it.'"

Major Tidwell Ingram, the massive sheriff's bailiff, was a political activist with clout. Along with trial security, he oversaw communications between judge and jury.

The court only learned of the episode afterwards and according to administrators, "Though the judge, attorneys, deputies and court reporter are scattered throughout the building, we get the word to them. The judge would never violate the criminal code that jurors may request to examine physical evidence again."

"The law didn't allow taking notes," *said one juror to whom I spoke.* "We had difficulty remembering time frames the case hinged upon. Defense Attorney Greer had posters charting his claims to the minute."

Disillusioned jurors wondered why they were wringing their guts and bashing heads for what some viewed as a charade. Some feared repercussions. A juror misquoted Judge Boddie's verbal charge according to the law, "He instructed us that we had to be sure *beyond the shadow of any reasonable doubt.*"

Another juror argued, "No. That's wrong. He said, and the law is, we must be sure *beyond any reasonable doubt.*" Weariness continued and quick tempers flared as conflicting opinions crossed.

Chapter 37

Something Eerie

With Saturday morning slated for closing summations, a weekend verdict was expected. District Attorney Scott Taylor made his first appearance and some jurors seethed, "We had looked for him all week. It was an insult when he showed up for the big moment."

For the prosecution, Jack Eberlee went first and Emily Devreaux initiated the rebuttal. With his dark-rimmed glasses, Eberlee resembled a young Clark Kent hurrying between the witness stand and the counsel table to consult his notes.

Edwin Greer's fluid delivery stroked the egos of the twelve VIPs entrusted with his client's life. Usually Harvard-groomed, he hadn't shaved and his stubbled chin, fatigue lines and red-rimmed eyes suggested an all-night vigil in his motel room.

"Ivrin Bolden is twenty-three years old, has led an exemplary, honorable life. The state wants to take that life from him, imprison him for the rest of his life—without benefit of probation, parole or suspension. If you convict him of second-degree murder, the sentence is automatic. Few people in their lives have an occasion to determine the rest of the years of a fellow human being. You will determine whether he is able to overcome this nightmare and make something of his remaining years. This was a tragic incident. Brenda Spicer and her family deserve your sympathy. If you could bring Brenda Spicer back, you would. If I could bring her back, I would..."

Who would believe it except the 100 or so spectators jamming the courtroom? Something eerie—indelible on the mind—interrupted Greer. Overcast skies matched the mood in the courtroom with side windows raised slightly to relieve the humidity. A gusty wind rattled the Venetian blinds in clattering dissent, reminiscent of another storm, another defense attorney, another bizarre tragedy.

Greer resumed, "If Ivrin Bolden could bring Brenda Spicer back..." *The wind made an absurd left turn toward the front of the courtroom and the American flag in its brass stand clanged to the floor. A deputy ran to close the windows and right the flag. Torrents of rain beat phantom fists against the panes. Nature's inexplicable tantrum hung a pall of sobriety and uneasiness over the summation.*

Greer continued his impassioned deportment. "…a greater tragedy would be to convict an innocent man. And Brenda Spicer doesn't want that responsibility. You would do her no favor. To convict, the defendant must be found guilty beyond *every* reasonable doubt. Look at a few of those doubts. These posters may help you."

In comparison to the state's earlier generalized presentation, the posters were pinpointed. "The state's theory is implausible. It could not have happened the way they claim. No bruises or scratches on Brenda's buttocks. You heard police testimony that the concrete floor of the small three or four-foot space (police had measured the unit as six-by-nine) was dusty and dirty. They said it could have happened standing up, done neatly. No evidence on Ivrin's clothes, scratches or bruises on him. The halftime theory is impossible—every time he didn't have a bunch of witnesses around, the state says that's when it happened. Think about Zachary Gil's strange testimony, the doubt about a relationship between him and Miss Spicer. The service couldn't identify Ivrin. Zachary Gil matches their description better. Another unreasonable doubt: no unusual demeanor or behavior at the basketball game. If you lived a good life as you all have, then committed a violent crime, wouldn't it show?"

If angels wept, I thought, he'd be drowning in saltwater.

"Ivrin had no motive. Brenda Spicer was out of the picture. Joel would graduate and get a job where he could see her all the time. So would Ivrin, a peaceful, law-abiding guy, take this strong measure? Brenda Spicer was alone in the house in Jena. He could have gone there. At NLU with everybody around was an illogical time and place. He's been accused of a lot, but not of being stupid. People were driving by the warehouse. Driving back to campus with a body in his car? He wanted to help the police and cooperated with them. A lot we don't know about Brenda Spicer. She carried a gun, took late night walks, dated Zachary Gil's brother and others. Her killer, an ex-boyfriend or maybe her brother, is still out there watching, hoping you'll convict an innocent man."

He took his seat. The vocal juror whistled half under his breath and then opined, "Now that guy's a lawyer. If I'm ever put on trial, that's who I'd want."

Chapter 38
Impugning Words

Devreaux rebutted, "Who had the most to gain by killing Brenda Spicer? Who stood in the best light by her death? She was grating on Ivrin Bolden's nerves and he killed her. By January, he felt he had lost his girl, taken from him by Brenda Spicer. The theory of the state's case, how we...we feel it happened. She met the defendant in front of the police department at about 5:45, 5:50. Ivrin was going to meet her there so he could give...get some film...a camera from her."

She pushed on, "Now Bolden said...'Come with me to the storage.' She said okay, she knew him, they had talked to each other, they knew who they were. She went with him, followed him inside. He grabbed her by the neck like Dr. McCormick said, broke the two wish bones in her neck." Re-enacting the murder, Devreaux grasped her throat and staggered backward, "We're talking about a three-foot space."

Unbelieveable, I thought, she had repeated what I'd learned were Greer's mistaken dimensions of a crawl space in an attic.

"And when a tall person grabs a short person, they're going to fall back.

She tried to grab the wall or something to catch herself. He's strangling her and she doesn't have a chance to grab him; he snaps her neck and in a minute's time, she was dead." It was Devreaux's finest moment. She had tears in her eyes. One female juror pursed her lips and stared at her lap.

"When a person dies, they can't fight. Their brain isn't working, their heart isn't pumping blood and with her body relaxed on the floor, he raped her. There aren't any bruises on her back. Of course not, but she was definitely lying on that dusty concrete floor. Look at her blouse—in the front, the colors are sharp, in the back, it's dusty and light colored. Why wasn't her vagina or rectum torn? Because she's dead. She's given it all she can give. He probably took his pants off and laid them in a clean area. He went back to Harris Hall and alibied himself. Of course, his behavior hadn't changed. Acting nervous would have brought suspicion, so he acted just as you see him doing now. But he acted differently yesterday. You saw him get angry when I questioned him. When he isn't under stress, he laughs and jokes as he has throughout this trial. This is serious. It doesn't have any effect on him.

"At the halftime he hit the first trash bin at Northeast Louisiana University, because her body was trash and he wanted to get rid of it. The state's theory of this case...it's not really a theory...just what the evidence has shown...that Brenda Spicer died. You know that. And the evidence has shown beyond a reasonable doubt that Ivrin Bolden killed her and it's quite possible, very possible...in fact definite he killed her at his warehouse. We know she had some problems. At NLU, Joel Tillis kind of took her in, was like a sister and very close friend. Their friendship grated on the defendant's nerves. He and his lawyer used the words 'a difference of opinion,' 'a disagreement' and 'tension.' If he made his dislike subtle, no one would suspect he hated her. He admitted sending her a letter, 'Quit following Joel around like a whipped puppy. Leave her alone or I'll handle it.' Weigh the testimony of Joel Tillis and her mother. I submit they didn't tell the truth. Joel gets her doctor husband. Her mother gets her A-okay son-in-law."

Barred from the courtroom on the chance of a recall, Joel hovered by the door in the foyer. Eavesdropping in view of the bailiff, she overheard

Devreaux impugning her word. A court clerk who walked by said, "She was mad as spit, stomping her feet, cursing and disagreeing. I don't know who the show was for, but it was a good one."

Fearful they'd miss the verdict, spectators lunched on vending machine snacks. Three lawyers held cocktail court at a tavern. "Hey, to me *supernatural* means a woman without any silicone. But if I'd been Greer, when that flag hit the deck, I'd have recessed for a rosary. That wind did a ninety-degree wheelie and roared like a motorcycle toward the front. Everybody saw it. Nobody wants to talk about it."

Chapter 39

Guilty
or Innocent?

The verdict came after three hours. Undercurrents crackled like hot wires and Judge Boddie instructed, "After the reading of the verdict, please remain seated and maintain order until after we dismiss the jury."

Reporters flipped their notebooks to fresh pages. The jury filed in with tears streaming down the faces of several women. Downcast as prisoners linked in a chain gang, they stared at the neck of the one ahead.

"Have you reached a verdict?"

The jury foreperson tilted her chin, "We have, Your Honor. The jury finds Ivrin Bolden *not guilty*."

Stunned silence exploded into jubilant rooting. The Bolden family praised God, exchanged group hugs and pumped hands. Others shook their heads, "I can't believe it. This is wrong, wrong, wrong." Some cried while others comforted them. Ivrin looked joyless and absorbed, accepting handshakes like a man eating a steak before his execution. Hands in his pockets, he surveyed the happy supporters and the gloomy dissenters.

Judge Boddie released the jury while spectators waited as instructed.

Then, an off-the-wall scene riveted the courtroom. The foreperson rose from her chair weeping openly. As the others filed slump-shouldered through the exit, she hung left, stretched out her arms as though entranced and walked toward the defense table.

A hush fell and conversations dropped mid-sentence. When the juror extended both arms to embrace Ivrin's mother, she drew back in startled reflex, as though expecting a slap. Judge Boddie did a circular roll in his chair. Devreaux stared in revulsion.

She locked eyes with Ivrin a few feet away and started toward him to congratulate him. Something stopped her and she approached Devreaux instead, "I know how hard you worked. You did a fine job, but we couldn't convict on the case presented."

"If you only knew," said Devreaux and turned her back in disgust. The foreperson's actions drew as much talk as the nude inmate dubbed "The Streaker" who had once raced gleefully through the courtroom wearing only socks with deputies in pursuit.

Edwin Greer looked somber. He exchanged legal etiquette with Devreaux and Eberlee.

Watching Greer, I wondered if he longed to take the two young attorneys so bruised by the outcome to a dim bar to comfort them.

He told the press, "I never doubted the outcome. The verdict came as no surprise because Ivrin was…simply innocent."

District Attorney Scott Taylor gave a statement: "We knew it was going to be a tough case to win. But we believed the evidence compelled it going to trial. The jury has spoken."

In the foyer, Joel screamed, did a cheerleader leap and waited for Ivrin to filter through the mob. Vindication was Joel's as well. Sissy, Wendy and Sara talked in funeral monotones when she approached to resume their friendship where the murder had interrupted it. Sara shook her head, "Joel, I have nothing good to say to you."

"Aw, come on, now." They hugged the wall in contempt.

Emotional and gesturing, the foreperson told reporters, "The state didn't prove its case." Driving home, she puzzled over locking eyes with Ivrin—not the gratitude she had expected—surely a wrong interpretation.

Ivrin's mother, after treating Joel as an adored fiancée for a year, flounced past her in the corridor. Their unity had served its purpose, and she was the predator again who had ruined Ivrin's life. Joel ducked into the bathroom to check her makeup. The snobs and hypocrites would never break her. The last time she had cried was at Brenda's funeral.

Chic in a navy and grey shoulder-padded suit and wearing dark sunglasses, Joel posed with Ivrin on the courthouse steps and emoted for cameras, disputing the trial with indignant motions. The media regained control of their interviews by shifting microphones to the one actually acquitted. Ivrin studied the sidewalk with a broad grin, "I have no hard feelings toward the prosecution or anyone. I'm glad the ordeal's over. Glad I'm free. I knew I didn't commit murder so I felt confident. I just want to get out of Monroe, start my life again and resume school."

His defense reportedly cost $90,000. Causey said, "I heard his mother canceled a new Mercedes she had ordered. Life is just chockfull of tragedy."

Joel didn't hear the predictions, "God help her. She'll be next."

Looking over at the statue of Lady Justice in the park across from the courthouse, blindfolded and balancing the scales, it was pockmarked by weather, stained by the excrement of pigeons.

Taylor agreed to my interview. The reception accorded me by his secretary was so sugary I imagined my shoes sticking to the floor. A staff investigator passed the blame, "If there was anything lacking, it was up to the police and Ms. Devreaux to fill in any blanks." *The blanks were many and he denied responsibility.* "I know you're a nice lady who doesn't want to hurt anybody. That you'll keep it clean. Everybody did their jobs. Bolden just lucked out."

He and his secretary exchanged glances I would see many times: Well, how do you think it went?

A female juror said in our meeting, "I believed absolutely in Ivrin's innocence from day one. I told my husband early on he wasn't guilty. He was nice and refined, well-dressed and brought a briefcase to court—seemed more like a lawyer than a murderer."

"Months later," *she went on,* "I awoke, bolted upright in bed and decoded what I felt I had seen in Ivrin's eyes: 'Well, I got away with it.'"

Chapter 40
Dark Reflections

In Jena, I sat on the patio with Brenda Spicer's mother, drinking coffee. "My daughter needed no defense nor do we. If her father or brothers could have slipped a gun into the courtroom, they would have leveled Ivrin. Would the verdict have been different if we had put on a sideshow, too?"

My investigation and justice for the victim seemed dead. I couldn't accuse an innocent man. The case lingered in Monroe like a ghostly fog. Insiders who had ducked having to testify had depended on others to trumpet the cause and for Bolden's luck to run out. Those who, by omission, had abetted him took solace in clichés: the mind of the sociopath is its own furnace. Law enforcement knew better: ocean breezes and frigidity of soul fanned those without pity or remorse. Psychiatrists, attorneys and courts had often held that madness was blameless.

Interviewing students, I bought enough pizza to feed Italy. Wendy broke down. Her eyes questioned, "How much do you know about me? How much should I tell you? How far can I trust you?" *When leaving, she said unnecessarily,* "I promised this cute guy I'd pick him up from work and we'd go out."

One August afternoon, Wendy and I sat on my boat dock sipping lemonade—trapped in the silence of nothing moving. The bayou was empty of swimmers and boats, insects glided on noiseless wings, even turtles and swamp birds had retreated to the silt bottom or the willow shade. No one in the universe but this girl and I with half-pretense and half-trust hanging between us. Her cheekbones were angular in her denim cut-offs and sleeveless tee; she looked skinny and edgy.

Engaged in mental pole fishing, she nibbled at my questions before jerking back and leaving the hook empty. I needed to corroborate the intimations made in court. She sank low in the lawn chair, "Yes, Brenda and Joel were lovers. Prosecutors didn't ask the witnesses who knew about it direct questions."

I didn't feel good at robbing her of allegiance.

Part 2

New Orleans

Chapter 41

Slashing Each Other

For many New Orleans transplants, the promise of the city was getting lost and making a fresh start. A foreign country on the edge of the Southern United States with its Old World mystique, urban aloofness and live-and-let-live philosophy, oddity was normal and went unnoticed.

With their cheap, rutted lifestyle, the promise failed for Joel and Ivrin. The past was still their present, with one difference—she noticed a new intensity in his stare, as though she were some unidentified bacteria beneath a microscope.

Joel rehashed the trial and took sweeping bows for her role. "It's just you and me, no cameras," Ivrin advised. "So pack it in. I need to reorganize and move ahead."

"I'd think you'd be happier about the outcome and more appreciative. You could help out around here and get a decent job." One moment she expected him to be outraged at the cops, the prosecutors, the traitor witnesses and his parents' treatment of her. The next he should be strewing rose petals in her path, because he wasn't in prison. "I lost my friends, my standing in Monroe, even job recommendations because of your crazy temper and jealousy."

"You conveniently forget, sweet tart, none of it would have happened except for you and Brenda."

They resembled cock fighters slashing each other in a horrid dance of vengeance. It took an argument to generate even lust and the bedroom became a charity ward to patch their wounds. Ivrin regressed to a child. Oblivious to seals of approval, he played video games and computer solitaire.

Their luxury weekends in New Orleans while in college were a bitter reminder of their now barren existence. The Crescent City in the shape of a slice of melon had turned flat and tasteless. Lake Ponchatrain's heady aura of seaweed and shrimp boats ploughing saltwater, pungent chicory coffee luring tourists to the French Market, world famous restaurants and sunsets riding the rim of the Gulf mocked their poverty. They had lost the passion, but mutual blackmail kept them together.

"The arguments are about everything," she told Tara and Cherise, "household chores, bills, his loafing around and his jealousy of my new friends."

Ivrin seethed over the skull-cracking boulders she held over his head, his failure to find work equal to his education and her gripes about his friends. She was his sole preoccupation, "Who did you go to lunch with today? Why are you so late getting home? Why do you want to go home to Hammond by yourself? What did Cherise Gates want?" Cherise listened to the daily serial of Lady Di and the Uncharming Prince.

Joel persisted, "I saved you, Ivrin, and I expect some concessions in return." The concessions were impossible, such as asking his parents for money and staying motivated though potential employers turned him away after background checks.

"I bring sodas and milk home and they evaporate. I'm not going to live this way, so what are you going to do? Get back into graduate school, join the Irish Republican Army or run for governor? You can't even make your spit balls stick to the wall. I'm not working and cleaning while you watch cartoons or you show off by helping your friend with medical courses you flunked. You use two or three towels when showering. What do you do, make love to them?" Joel's carping sounded as familiar as the hum of the refrigerator.

Lady Di was in debt, cut off from the royal allowance, stuck in a dismal flat and powerless. Walking to work, a picture of sultry, laughing Marie Labeaux, the legendary Voodoo Queen, drew Joel into a junk shop to leaf through a yellowed book on black magic. "The effigy may be destroyed, but its power lives on." The heavy musk of sassafras root and incense, thumping drums on a stereo and the dark probing eyes of a turbaned fortune-teller drove her back into the sunlight street. Her belief in life as a circle, she could not outrun the dead girl.

Ivrin's R.O.T.C. commission would restore his pride, bring order to his environment again, provide what they needed and leave his troubles behind. Joel hesitated giving up her career plans to play house frau on a military base. The dilemma solved itself when the Army said, "No thanks." Sprinkling rhinestones on the turndown, she told her family, "They decided it was too costly to activate Ivrin as an officer."

He asked, "What do you and Cherise find to talk about every day?" She must have seemed to cram Cherise down his throat as she had Brenda.

When she talked of leaving Ivrin, blackmail coiled in their voices. After a violent argument, she fled to Hammond. Believing she had done her part at his trial, her mother and grandmother begged her, "Get away from him. He's insane."

Tara counseled her long distance. "Why do you stay? You weren't raised to share the soap without marriage."

In college, Joel had settled on age twenty-five to marry Ivrin. With three more years to go, she ached to live her dreams before lugging babies and cellulite on her hips.

"The point is he's started hitting you." Tara wondered if Joel thought she deserved the abuse.

In May, she told Tara, "I have to get out of Louisiana. As long as I'm close by, he'll never let me alone."

Tara, doing well in her career, said, "Come to Memphis and stay with me until you can afford your own place. I have to pay rent, monthly bills and buy groceries anyway. You can find a job, sock some money away and not be dependent on anyone." Joel resigned from her job, scribbled a note telling Ivrin not to follow her and drove to Hammond to say goodbye to her family.

Part 3

Memphis

Chapter 42

New Town, Old Problems

Searching for employment, Joel found a manager trainee job for a women's shoe store. Tara's apartment, with its private lake, park, tennis courts and security gate, enthralled her. The setup was perfect—she worked days while Tara worked nights. They had privacy, enjoyed each other's company and Joel kept the apartment spotless. Ivrin often called with magnanimous ideas for shooting even higher than his botched medical career. Though his inability to forget her was flattering, she said, "Memphis is a fascinating city of opportunities and goal-oriented people. We are not getting back together."

At work, she blended into the airy spaces of the mall where palms and tropical flowers bloomed in atrium fountains and fashionable, sanguine women preened like exotic birds, flashing jewels and credit cards with scarlet talons. She struggled financially—her modest salary was another layaway plan until she could earn more. However, her bankrupt credit didn't subdue her rich taste. Joel urged Tara to buy her dream car, "You deserve it. You work hard and you're successful."

"Joel, I have other priorities: keeping my nieces and nephews in school clothes and paying for their music lessons and sports gear. If I get in over my head, I don't want to have to sleep in a fancy car."

With her first paycheck, Joel bought an expensive suit. "Tara, you should buy some gorgeous clothes."

Lounging in her work attire, Tara groaned, "I'm not a clothes horse. We can only wear one outfit at a time."

Tara didn't understand, nor did Joel, what kept her running harder and needing more. Nebulous knowing brushed her brain as frail wings then fluttered from her grasp.

Long-distance telephone charges mounted and Tara wondered about the unusual closeness between Joel and Cherise, who worked in the music industry. One Sunday, Tara overheard Joel tell her, "They preached about you in church today." What an odd thing to say. The sermon had been on homosexuality.

Joel switched to an interdenominational church that attracted young professionals. "Tara, you won't believe the people I've met; they own BMWs and condos at Gulf Shores. The pastor doesn't hang us with thou-shalt-nots. It's a positive message: we're put here to enjoy life and prosper."

"Joel, that's not a church; it's an Easter Parade. Spirituality isn't bragging about money and showing off expensive watches."

"You can be just as spiritual enjoying a nice life." On down days, Joel knew the last time she had seen God was in a country cemetery in Jena, and she had left Him there.

Living with Tara soon rubbed. Joel needed the ego stroke of letting everyone in Monroe—the city left in disgrace—know how fine her life was. Tara sat across from her at breakfast. "We need to talk about this ninety dollar phone bill. You can't operate on impulse and day rates." Joel gave her fifty dollars, her only contribution to free room and board in Dreamland.

Three months later, as though plucking her vulnerability from the airwaves, Ivrin shucked his mediocre job and moved to Memphis. When he came, Tara cleared the air, "Understand me. I won't compete with you over Joel. She's a friend; you're a boyfriend. Don't put me in the middle. You want time with her, I'm a ghost."

The telephone bill escalated. Their communication in college lost, the discussion turned to an argument. "Couldn't you work out a long-distance budget rather than call everybody on impulse? The point of moving in was to save some money, but you blow it before you make it. You can't keep doing this."

"Don't tell me what I can and cannot do, Tara. I don't have to put up with it!"

"I want to help you, but I'm not financing your talking to Cherise three times a day. Why do you still call all of those people in Monroe?"

"Fine, I'll move out. I'm taking an apartment with Ivrin."

He promised to rehang the moon and stars, restore the fun times and laughter. When friends asked why she moved in with him again, she said, "My friendship with Tara deteriorated. I had no other place to go." Self-reliant as she appeared, the four-year off-and-on union had left an indelible dependency. She needed a man for security—collection letters from her creditors arrived regularly.

She assured her family, "This is a test run to see if he's really changed." They would recapture the magic of fate tapping her on the shoulder when she had met him and had told friends, "He was sent from God to make me happy."

Friends tried to believe Joel's response to the timeworn question: *Is he guilty*? "Ivrin said he didn't kill Brenda and I believe him. He would never harm me. I know how to handle him."

Chapter 43

Explosions

Joel reasoned that Ivrin's best friend, like Brenda, had come between them. He saw how much she had changed during their brief separation. Renting an economical one-bedroom apartment, he took the first job offer with a security company that provided guards to businesses—temporary until landing something better. With his golden-boy façade still fading, the hard times were depressing and Joel reminisced about their Camelot years.

"That was my parents' money. I can't hide a diamond in a candy box and treat you like a movie star anymore."

Ambition regressed to malaise. He bought a remote control toy car for fifty dollars and spent hours racing it around the parking lot. She exploded, "I'm sick of your loafing and playing."

A weekend visit from Ivrin's best friend added to the tension and solidified her resolve to leave. Joel turned up the stereo to drown the mindless bleep of video games and she listened to motivational success tapes which fired her determination to make big money and buy happiness. Many newcomers to Memphis applied with a parcel delivery service. She dashed home after work and dolled up in a red suit and high heels. The corporate office already closed, she buttonholed a guy coming out and wrangled her way inside to make out a job application. He took her to dinner.

Joel's friend, Cherise Gates, asked, "Weren't you worried about going out with a stranger?"

"A stranger is just a friend you haven't met yet. You want to bet they hire me?"

Her secondary plan became a thirty-something man who was an executive she met at a seminar. He was urbane, good-looking, with business acumen—but married. They explored her options with his company.

In her leisure time, to enliven the grind of going to work and back home, Joel dashed off to meet her married friend or talk on the phone with Cherise and other gal-pals. Ivrin saw Brenda reincarnated in Cherise. If one said October 15 was Easter, the other would dye her eggs. It was Monroe repeated with rivalry poisoning the air. He complained, "You two can't even decide what to eat for breakfast without a thirty-minute yak session."

Ivrin and Cherise argued, "Get lost and stop butting in." She and Joel paid no attention.

She came home to the sink filled with dishes, clothes thrown on a chair and Ivrin playing with a puzzle toy. "I'm not working all day then cleaning up your mess. Why can't you be like my executive friend and apply yourself? My other friend is successful with a college degree and earns big money selling farm equipment."

"Don't compare me to other men. I'll decide what to do when I'm ready. It won't be because you pushed me into it."

"Oh right, I forgot. That's why your head's messed up, because your mama always pushed you." Slamming her on the floor, he pounded her with his fists. She received treatment for bruises and lacerations at a hospital emergency room. A co-worker gave her shelter.

Ivrin called her at work, "If you leave, it's without the car and with the clothes on your back. I'll tell your relatives, your boss, everybody about what happened in Monroe."

Joel went back. A few more months and she could leave. He tried harder—did laundry, vacuumed and bought burgandy silk bed sheets to reignite their romance. They attended church to get their lives back on track, but Joel soon quit and he gave up on it.

She and Tara reconciled. Basketball season triggered a yearning to see the Lady Indians play. Tara drove Joel to a road game two hours away. They arrived early and waited near the team bench while news of their presence spread through the locker room. "Everyone—Coach Davies, Coach Anderson and the players—hid in the dressing room," said Wendy. "Nobody wanted the embarrassment of acting as though nothing had changed. Finally, Coach Anderson bit the bullet and visited with them."

The attitude was pointed; they would still be there for her had she been there for Brenda. Tara, who was also popular while at Northeast Louisiana University, was unprepared for the chill and nudged Joel. "What's going on here? Why don't we leave and find a friendly Klan meeting?"

"I am not leaving! These bigots can shuck popcorn in hell." Sissy sent a note from the dressing room: "Tara, it isn't you. I'll explain later."

She wrote Tara a letter. "Joel was a sweet girl when she came to NLU. But when she covered for Ivrin, knowing he raped and killed Spicer, she burned her bridges."

Joel would show them all she believed in his innocence with a blowout wedding. She and Cherise made guest lists. "I'll have a red and white theme with hundreds of candles, a catered hotel reception and a ski honeymoon in Aspen. If his family doesn't attend, that's fine."

In the tone of a bill collector, Ivrin asked, "Joel, who's paying for this?" It hadn't occurred to her that refusing money from his parents included their wedding.

"I'm not standing in front of some justice of the peace, eating at a fast food place and having a theme park honeymoon."

He brooded. Her lavish plans were to impress others; spending their lives together wasn't the point. Joel broke the news to Cherise while he sprawled on the sofa watching sports. "We've called it off. I'm not getting married until I can have the kind of wedding and honeymoon I want and I'm not marrying Dr. Bolden until he decides to be somebody again. Get real. I'll never return my ring. I've paid for it in too many ways."

Ivrin vaulted across the room, tipped her and the kitchen stool to the floor and wrestled the diamond off her finger. Glaring at her broken nail, she called Cherise back, "He's showing off and took my ring. He'll just give it back." At a pawnshop where he had steadily sold his golf clubs, monogrammed luggage and chess set, he hocked the ring.

At night, his presence in the bed threw her into fitful imaginings. The blonde girl had moved into the apartment with them. "But there's no room," Joel begged. "You know what he'll do!" She walked with the girl again along the bayou reflecting the moon, inhaling sweet jasmine, talking until daybreak, swapping secrets and souls. "He'll never know I'm here," the girl said. The reverie ended when Joel reached over to hug her, but it was only the man, the killer of love and innocence.

When Ivrin worked evenings, Joel's date took her dancing or to a movie. Tara asked, "Joel, are you nuts? You don't date one man while living with another. Ivrin will find a way to off him without being caught. Do the guy a favor; don't pull him into this."

"Ivrin and I have an understanding he can no longer control me." She went on a diet and bought only rice cakes and health food. A few more months of stashing some money and finishing her women's shoe store trainee program, she could bail out. Her trim figure would attract suitable men.

Plan B was her married friend getting her into training for a business franchise where he said she could rack up big bucks compared to retail.

Tara called Cherise. "Maybe you can reason with her. Ivrin is tracking her every move. And get this. To shake him up, after aerobics, she was looking hot in pink tights and yellow shorts. Spotting this hunk in the parking lot, she introduced herself and dragged him inside the apartment for a soda—knowing Ivrin was home. They're getting acquainted when he comes out of the bedroom, sits on the sofa and stares at them. The new guy glanced at Ivrin—who's-he-and-what-am-I-doing-here? Joel waved her hand, 'Oh, that's my boyfriend.' That poor dude guzzled his drink, shook hands and probably left town. "

"Joel doesn't need more control, Tara."

Pushing the right buttons didn't bring the predictable reaction anymore. Joel saw dead cold in Ivrin's eyes. His security job assigned him to guard duty at Graceland and his fascination with the white-pillared, palatial home of legendary singer Elvis Presley seemed as predictable as blood in a Stephen King novel. The nouveau riche melancholy with shuttered windows blocking sunlight and the hodgepodge décor of formal scarlet furniture, an electronic game room with gaudy fabric ceilings, the macabre Hawaiian Room of stuffed cockatoos, monkeys and island furnishings, seemed to be a search for identity. Reveling in the importance of guarding the vintage automobiles, the trophy room of costumes and gold records, in addition to the rose garden cemetery with its legacy of untimely death, Ivrin invited acquaintances to visit as though he lived there.

In their lethal maneuvers, Joel searched his dresser and personal belongings and found a letter from his best friend. She told Tara, "It said things one man shouldn't be saying to another man." She saw the letter as a bargaining tool for leaving without repercussions and confronted him, "I'm sending it to your snobby mother!"

He twisted Joel's arm behind her back and grappled the letter. "Shut up about my mother! You still have your family."

"That's okay. I made a dozen copies. And you broke with your family long before me."

In their ongoing argument about the letter, she insulted his parents again and told the emergency room doctor in regard to her injury, "I fell while jogging and sprained my wrist."

Tara, though nervous, took her in temporarily. Ivrin called daily begging her to come back. "I'm sorry. Things will be different." *Don't make me tell what I know about you*, he probably thought.

She went back. Tara met Ivrin for lunch and took a light approach, "When are you two going to stop banging your high chairs and throwing diapers at each other?"

He ducked his head and grinned, "I've learned one thing. I'll never let myself love any woman the way I did her." Tara noticed he had used the past tense about loving Joel.

Tara reasoned with her, "Why would he keep an incriminating letter? You carry your checkbook, bills and diary to work. So you know he's going through everything when you're gone. He knows you're doing the same. Maybe he wanted you to find it."

"I've told him that I'm cutting out when I finish my trainee program. To keep him from shafting my career, I've put the truth about what happened in Monroe on a disk and given it to a friend to be turned over to the police if anything happens to me. He doesn't want it falling into the wrong hands."

"Joel, don't make threats without following through. If you haven't given someone a copy, you should." Tara knew her too well. Like confessors on Death Row, she would save the whole truth for the cyanide drop. Only if dead did she want it known.

Joel's old, high mileage car with engine problems was repossessed—a knockout punch, her last semblance of self-reliance gone. Ivrin transported her to work and home again when he wasn't working. Often she walked or rode the bus, counting the weeks until her escape.

Chapter 44

Crashing Down

Ivrin's security company temporarily assigned him to guard duty at a plant in Arkansas where union workers were on strike. He brooded over what Joel did in his absence.

Homesickness tugged at Joel. She asked her date to drive her to Spring Fever at Northeast Louisiana University—a hedonistic unwinding before final exams with mud volleyball, rock concerts, canoe races, beer busts and shrimp boils. She showed off her handsome and toned date. "Life is great. I'm happy. Sorry I've lost touch, but my career's skyrocketing."

Some were civil and Brenda wasn't mentioned. Sara rounded a corner in Brown Hall and almost bypassed the familiar looking woman. "Joel, is that you? I can't believe it. You're a bone." Sara figured her a size four, older looking. Beneath the bubbly act she seemed moody and dejected.

"Yeah, it's me. I'm running and doing aerobics."

"How is Ivrin doing?"

"I haven't talked to him." True. Though still living together, they weren't speaking.

Resenting Joel's haughtiness, Sissy Burke tried to scare her. "This lady in Monroe is writing a book about Brenda's murder and interviewing us. I can't wait to read it."

Starstruck, Joel shared the news with Tara, "Joel, you act as though you want it told."

Ivrin learned Joel's date had gone with her to NLU and to Hammond to meet her family and requested emergency time off from his job in Arkansas. Highway 90, running through the isolated countryside of Forrest City merged with the interstate thirty miles from Memphis. Forrest City was a small town and Sheriff Dave Parkman was working late. With a drawl unhurried as a mountain creek, he defied stereotypes of a rube sheriff and was reelected every four years. His staff of ten and his single investigator, Glenn Ramsey, had wrapped up a tough week: a combine stolen from a cotton gin, a honky-tonk shooting, school vandalism, a rash of thefts. He and the man speeding across the bridge toward Memphis would meet.

With his suitcase barely in the door, Ivrin and Joel argued over her taking another man to Monroe and Hammond. The trip to Monroe was their last date. Something scared Joel's date off and he got an unlisted telephone number.

Joel went out three nights in a row supposedly with the girls from work. Ivrin paced the floor, then lay on the sofa in the dark and at 4:00 A.M., he heard her key and turned on the lamp. Rather than tired, she looked dreamy-eyed.

"Where have you been?" he asked.

She brushed past him, "At my executive friend's office going over sales brochures. I have to work days, you know."

Tara warned her to cool it. Joel argued, "This guy is the man Ivrin used to be. We're just close friends. He's intelligent and supportive with drive..."

"And married. If he were my husband hanging out all night with you, I'd tell him he'd listened to that poor girl's troubles long enough."

Joel doubted Ivrin's excuse that his security job had laid him off, but he refused to discuss it. "Now that you've lost another job, how are we supposed to pay rent and utilities and buy groceries? I have to handle the car note and insurance."

"Thanks to you and Spicer, Monroe rides my back when I apply for a good job. You rub my nose in it with dates and married friends." He slammed her against the wall.

"Do anything to me and my computer disk goes to the cops." Ivrin grabbed his keys and drove to the arcade. Joel walked to work, heavy in her steps, humidity souring her hair and melting her makeup.

His paranoia intensified. She was making too much noise, involving too many people and taking the phone into the bedroom when Cherise called. He couldn't crack her computer password to see if her exposé really existed.

On Mother's Day weekend, Ivrin refused to let Joel take the car and insisted on driving her to Hammond for the weekend. Relatives complimented her slim figure and new hairstyle. He spoke of exciting job interviews.

Back in Memphis, everything told her to run, run now. She had wild thoughts that Brenda, dead for two years, was either guiding her to safety or lulling her to complacency. Without her car, she couldn't leave town. He might even barge into the store and get her fired or carry tales to her married friend.

To Ivrin, it must have seemed that he could almost smell her wolf-like appetite for altercation. Joel said, "Let's go to the health club and work out." In a public place, he couldn't make a scene. On the handball court, an echo chamber of venomous rivalry, they slammed the ball with fury and had to keep playing until Ivrin won.

In the exercise room mirror, she glanced approvingly at her ribs arched above her flat belly and loosened her hair from a sweatband. Ivrin's eyes slid over her—devoid of desire. She was as readable as a scoreboard tabulating their mind games. Her self-improvement regimen was not for him.

Ivrin's hair glistened, his shirt and tennis shorts streaked with sweat and he waited. Straddling a weight press bench, she said, "I want to talk to you." Joel's expression was haughty and she treated him like a doleful kid soiling his Sunday pants and trying to smell invisible. Pulling a towel across the back of his neck in a seesaw motion, he asked, "About what?"

"I found some pictures in your winter jacket in the back of the closet. I want to know why."

"I kept them to...substitute when you turn me away. I want them back."

"I'm keeping them."

Their stalemate was a barbed wire fence keeping the other at bay. Her manager at the women's shoe store, Kaylee Conway, counseled, "Joel, stop hauling the baggage to work. You come in irritable and depressed and tee off easily."

After hours, Joel's married friend took her to see clients. He could slide her career to third base and replace Ivrin. All it would take was her wishful thinking and his divorce.

Ivrin reminded her, "You came into this world with nothing, sweets. You go out of it with nothing."

Out of character, Joel started keeping a diary of dates, times, places, who she saw, called it "Joel's bible" and guarded it. Another diary had almost been Ivrin's undoing. It would ward him off for two more weeks until she finished her work program.

At 10:30 P.M., after he left for his new security guard job, Joel called her married friend. "I need to talk. Can you pick me up?" With Ivrin wilder by the day, Joel needed to warn her married friend somehow without scaring him off. They sat on the marshmallow leather sofa in his office—the intense, mysterious woman engulfed in intrigue and seeking advice and the handsome executive who devoted personal time to his sales people. She listened to soul-baring blues on the stereo and recounted the death of her best friend, Ivrin's jealousy of their closeness. "They arrested him and we went through a long ordeal together."

He whistled softly, "Do you think he did it?"

"I felt he had something to do with it. When I asked him point-blank, he didn't answer. I thought that was odd if he didn't kill Brenda. He wasn't worried and the lawyers got him off. I moved in with him when he followed me here, because my friendship with Tara soured and I had no other place to go. He's consumed by knowing who I'm with every minute. I kept hoping he would snap out of it, but he's not going to change. I need to leave and get my own place."

He wondered what Joel expected of him: talk her into leaving him, give her a loan to get settled or be her solution. He was too busy, married and mortgaged to stash her in a hideaway or trade knuckles with a dangerous lover. She had a family who could help her. He advised her to pull available funds together and make her move. He drove her back to the apartment and headed home to explain to his wife why his business meeting had lasted until the bakery trucks hit the streets.

In the morning, Joel woke to Ivrin's long shadow superimposed against the sunlit drapes. His silence chilled her. Jumping from bed, she walked quickly toward the bathroom, throwing her words lightly over her shoulder. "I need to keep the car today."

"I'll take you to work. I have things to do." To keep a bird from flying, you clip its wings.

It was all coming down too fast. That afternoon, a co-worker drove Joel to the bank where she moved her small savings into her personal checking account and emptied her's and Ivrin's joint savings account.

Chapter 45

Another Victim

The arguments between Joel and Irvin went on and on, "You want your filthy pictures back, let me use my car or I'll mail them straight to your mother along with the disk."

"Give them to me, Joel. Then you can take the car."

Borrowing time, she said, "I'm hungry. I'm going to get something to eat." She grabbed Ivrin's keys, he followed her to the car and jumped into the passenger seat. At the fast food drive-thru window, she ordered breakfast. In the rush, he'd left his wallet, "Will you order something for me?"

"You want food? Buy it."

He had given her everything and she wouldn't even buy him a sausage biscuit. Ivrin grabbed the food bag and tossed it out the window. Hysterical, she tried to slap him and they drove home. He followed her into the bedroom and she yelled, "There's a store opening in Raleigh. I'm leaving tomorrow."

"Oh yeah? By hitchhiking or on a skateboard?"

Joel pulled the trump card that had always worked, "And I'm leaving with a guy I've been with before." His eyes narrowed to slits and she saw only hatred in them. Mind racing, she thought of one more button to push, grabbed the telephone and called Cherise. Almost incoherent, she begged, "I need you to come and pick me up. Now!"

"My car's on the fritz. Joel, what's going on..."

Later, his next steps would seem clear to others. Ivrin unplugged the cord. The universe exploded. There would always be another Brenda or Cherise, married guys or new dates, another letter or set of pictures. He could destroy them all and she would find replacements. He grabbed her arms, he slammed her onto the bed, gripped her throat and cut off her screams. He had seen the same terror in Spicer's face. He felt the bones in her neck snap and she ceased kicking. Convulsions shuddered through her body and her expression turned to resignation. Blood ran down her jaw and onto the sheets—red on burgundy. He heard the death rattle in her windpipe.

The act confirmed the research of Park Dietz, a forensics psychiatrist and FBI consultant who said, "Fifty-eight percent of repeat killers strangle their victims. It's a very personal, intimate means to feel their victims expire, see their convulsions, hear their last efforts to breathe. They are controlled, calculated, cunning offenders sexually aroused by their bloody handiwork. The victims are objects, sexual props, not people."

When Cherise called Joel she got only busy signals. *Other people, including myself, would theorize his next steps.* He removed Joel's uniform shirt with the store logo—too easy to identify. If wearing only her black bra, it might've pointed to a sexual attack. He shoved her new sneakers on her feet rather than her recognizable uniform shoes.

As Ivrin raced downstairs and backed the car trunk to the stairwell, he spotted K-9 dogs and a police squad banging on doors in another building and almost bolted. Casually, he walked back upstairs, wrapped Joel in the sheets and stuffed her in the closet.

On the balcony watching the raid, he must have been transfixed by the knowledge of Joel lying dead in his apartment while the police were sniffing for drugs. The police emerged with two guys handcuffed, loaded the dogs and residents drifted back inside. Checking the landing, some were to say Ivrin carried the body over his shoulder like a rolled-up rug. One of Greer's twelve reasonable doubts in the Brenda Spicer trial was Ivrin's inability to lift Brenda and throw her in the dumpster.

Later, police speculated that Ivrin sped over the state line into Arkansas and found the dumping place already picked out. If she were found, before a local cop connected her to someone missing from Memphis, he would be gone.

Spring, the season of love, red clover along highways, May sun coppering the Mississippi river, police figured on a back road Ivrin scanned the rearview mirror, slid the bundle down an incline and banked it with brush and goldenrod for camouflage. A few more yards to the dry ditch by the lake and she might have washed away in a rainstorm, but he was fighting time. He would hang around a couple of weeks, let the cops shoot their blanks and move to Florida.

Chapter 46
Déjà Vu

A t 1:40 P.M., Kaylee Conway, the women's shoe store manager, frowned. Joel often ran late, depending on whether "The Jerk" drove her or she walked. As business picked up, Kaylee grew irritated. Another lovers' spat or car trouble. She expected Joel to walk in with some creative excuse.

Repeatedly getting the glib recording, Cherise telephoned the store and told Kaylee, "Please, something is seriously wrong. She begged me to come and get her. I heard a struggle and the line went dead. Could you send someone to check on her?"

"We're shorthanded, but if she doesn't show soon, I will." She hesitated involving an employee.

Joel's married male friend also called. "This is peculiar," said Kaylee. "Too many people are looking for her." Alice Foster, a co-worker of Joel's, drove to the apartment and reported back, "No one's home and the car is gone. Security guard opened up and searched it. No sign of a problem."

As usual, Ivrin called the store around eight to ask if Joel needed a ride home. Kaylee was alarmed, "She didn't come in. We've been trying to reach her all afternoon."

"I dropped her off for work around noon at the mall entrance. She was in a huff this morning, said she was moving to Raleigh and wasn't coming back. Could you cover her shifts until I can find her?"

Around ten, Kaylee and Alice knocked on the apartment door. Ivrin answered with an unruffled go-away expression, "Joel isn't home."

"We want to come in."

"Look, I don't know where she is. It's late."

Foster said, "I swear I heard him laughing after he closed the door."

Tara, warding off the unthinkable, tried calming Cherise. "You know Joel. Maybe she's just pitching a bitch. She'll show up. Not on his wildest tantrum would Ivrin repeat himself."

"She wouldn't throw her job away."

Sounding blasé, Ivrin called Tara, "Have you heard from Tillis? We had a tiff and she didn't come home last night. Is she chillin' with you?"

Careful. Play it close. Glancing at the patio, Tara envisioned Joel lounging there last summer with her stereo. "Maybe she stayed with a co-worker."

"I've already checked; she didn't go to work, either. Do you think she could be with her married friend?"

"I can't see him taking her home to the wife and kids and stashing her in the guest room." Nor could she imagine Ivrin bold enough to repeat himself. Lightning never struck twice in the same place or so the old wives' tale went.

The next morning after receiving busy signals and voicemails, Kaylee finally got through, "Ivrin, have you heard from Joel yet?"

"No, she still isn't back, not a word."

She made a note: "Seems unconcerned. He muffled a giggle."

Cherise finally reached him. "No, I thought she was with you."

"You're lying. I heard a struggle before the phone went dead. I'm calling the Memphis police to report her missing."

"No. Let me do it." Joel had been gone thirty-one hours and Ivrin told Missing Persons, "She's probably visiting a friend."

Cherise hesitated worrying Joel's mother prematurely, but she had to know. "What do you mean missing? Where's Ivrin? Nobody's seen her since Thursday?" Joel's mother's fear raced in circles. "Tell me exactly what went on, what he said and how he's acting."

"He didn't even notify the police until I said I would. We're all frantic but he acts bored."

Premonition pounded the chest of Joel's mother: Whatever had happened had already happened. Hope clutched at frail branches: her daughter was dead; her daughter was alive; she wouldn't leave without a word.

Ivrin called the shoe store again, "Did she apply for a store near Raleigh? That's where she said she was going."

"Absolutely not," said Kaylee. "I hadn't assigned her to a manager's post yet."

Joel's married friend, out-of-town on business, telephoned his wife and she relayed a message, "Ivrin Bolden called and asked if you'd heard from Joel. He says she's missing, that no one's heard from her since Thursday."

The friend shut his briefcase and dropped back on the bed staring at the ceiling. "Not since Wednesday. They were having problems and she wanted to leave, so I guess she did."

Scarcely aware of the drive home, he wanted the story firsthand. "Ivrin, what's this about Joel?"

"She's gone. I thought you might have heard from her."

Joel's friend told the police, "When I pressed him about why Joel might have left, he admitted they had argued but said it was minor, no reason for her to go away and stay."

Joel's mother and sister arrived at the Memphis Police Department and told them, "He knew what time to expect us, but he had left to referee a ballgame like nothing had happened. He spent Mother's Day in my home. Now I'm the last person he wants to see."

The missing person report astounded her. "This is all wrong. Joel doesn't have an Afro. Even the clothes are wrong, she would have been wearing her uniform. She's six-feet, not five-eight." Ivrin's devilish lampoon registered with Joel's sister: Brenda Spicer was five-foot-eight.

"He said he didn't have a picture of her, ma'am."

"Why, he has dozens, even a videotape of her graduation. He's a camera nut. I'll bring you one from the apartment."

Memphis—where the Lady Indians, the love triangle and Brenda's murder meant nothing—was neutral ground without media focus. Joel's mother had no choice but to tell authorities about the coincidence of Ivrin's proximity in a similar case. "At the time, I didn't believe he killed Brenda Spicer."

Coincidences are reliable stoolies. Major Rodney Moore and Sergeant Blaire Donnor of Missing Persons thought the last person to see two women before they vanished warranted a hard look-see.

On the drive back to Hammond, numbness gave way to enmity and anguish and Joel's mother told her younger daughter, "Joel had to do things her way." Rain peppered the hood and the dark skyline of pine trees which were giant stalks. On the deserted shore of the Mississippi, an oil slick from a runaway barge ate the white sand. As they wept, the windshield wiper stroked the glass, "Hush, hush."

Some thought the news was too Hollywoodish to entertain, a Tillis production, a publicity stunt to land a sportscaster job, get on the *Oprah Winfrey Show* or put Ivrin in jail for a few weeks.

Sergeant Donnor searched the apartment. The absence of letters or bills made no sense. People with a permanent address left a paper trail. Fingers galloping over the keyboard, she faxed Monroe authorities for a copy of Ivrin Bolden's files and contacted Detective Bill Causey.

"I can't say I'm surprised. We felt he was guilty. I'll be very surprised if she's still alive. Go twenty miles in any direction and you'll find her. Oh and try the garbage dumpsters."

Bill Causey turned to Ricky Peel, "Fasten your seat belt. I got a call from Memphis PD. Joel Tillis vanished a week ago from her apartment where she'd been living with you-know-who. I expected him to throw a hair dryer into her bath water, something original. Our case is dead, but we can save them footwork on theirs."

Chapter 47

Media Circus

My vacation to Tampa, Florida, ended early when a friend called and read me the newspaper coverage of Joel Tillis's disappearance. The violent saga of Brenda Spicer's murder repeated itself with another media circus.

Sergeant Blaire Donnor phoned Ivrin twice a day, "Have you heard from Miss Tillis? No? Well, I kind of guessed not."

At the women's shoe store, Kaylee told Donnor, "He had the grits to try and pick up her paycheck. So he must not be expecting her back."

"Each time we brought him in," said Donnor, "He came cursing, kicking and screaming and stuck to his story."

In another interview, Major Rodney Moore said, "Mr. Bolden, neighbors say you and Miss Tillis had frequent arguments. Have you talked to her family since her disappearance? You haven't called us for progress reports, only to try and get your car back from impoundment."

"Her family has called me. I don't have to call you. You call me every day," Ivrin said.

"Joel's mother said you weren't on speaking terms with your parents.

But after our interview, you called them and they sought legal advice. For a man whose girlfriend is missing, you seem undisturbed. Instead of hostility, I'd think you'd want to help us."

Ivrin jumped up from the chair, "I have a lawyer. You cops tail me everywhere. I'm not answering any more questions."

"Fine, you're free to go. Just don't go too far."

"Cops don't scare me."

Moore drew a diagram of the mall and disputed Ivrin's story to Donnor, "No way Ivrin could drop her here and see her calling somebody. The only public phones are at the north entrance."

Ivrin complained to Tara Hester, "The police are hassling me. You know Joel; she's lying back somewhere laughing. I wouldn't tell this to anybody but you. They're even making accusations toward me because of some silly pictures Joel found."

Petrified, Tara told Cherise, "It was a ploy, feeling me out to see if I knew about the pictures and what I would say. He seemed satisfied, but I'm getting hang-up calls, as though he's checking to see if I'm home or trying to frighten me."

Ivrin didn't wait around to be strapped to another lie detector and borrowed three hundred dollars from Tara. She arranged for time off from work and she packed. "I'm going to visit my family. You can mail me a check at their address." When her police interview was done, she wanted Ivrin to think of her as unavailable to make any noise.

Ivrin smelled her fear. It was palpable. He offered to collect her mail from her security box in her absence. To allay suspicions that Joel had mailed her a copy of the disk, Tara gave him the key.

The apartment manager noticed a loaded moving van at Ivrin's apartment. Ivrin exited with his parents and they ignored the manager when she tried to stop him from skipping out on the lease. Except for Joel's clothes and dirty laundry, the place was stripped to the bare walls.

Ivrin mailed Tara a check and a thank you card.

The bread-butter-and-blood formality and his egocentric signature—

never merely Ivrin—sickened Tara. When she learned his parents had helped move Joel's furniture, jewelry and personal items, she called Cherise, "He lied about not checking my mail. The carrier dumps deliveries in batches. It was as organized as his desk in college."

The apartment manager called Shreveport to collect back rent and ask why Ivrin left so suddenly. Ivrin's mother said, "I've spoken to Joel's mother. She said some of Joel's friends have talked to her. She's alive, but ran away."

"Why would she do that?"

"She's a very dominant woman who always tried to rule Ivrin and get him to do what she wanted."

"What about the rent that's owed?"

"I'll let Joel's mother worry about the rent."

Ivrin's aunt in California, certain of his innocence the first time around, called Joel's mother. "She was stunned that Ivrin hadn't notified me and that I hadn't heard from him since. She must have faced him down because he called whining about being upset and pretending to care about me."

Joel's mother and sister returned to Memphis and packed Joel's clothes. Joel's sister saw stains resembling blood on jogging pants. Could he have put Joel's body in the closet until the drug bust was over?

Applying the heat, Donnor contacted Ivrin's father, "I want to know where your son is."

"He received a telephone call in the middle of the night. I believe from Joel...and he left for Florida to talk to her."

Yeah and I'm catching the red-eye to Mars, Donnor later told me he thought. "He was advised not to leave town, but you helped him move back home with you."

"I contacted a lawyer in Memphis and he was supposed to advise you Ivrin had left. Joel's mother has known all along she's in Florida. She's lying to the police and hiding her out."

"What reason would she have to do such a thing?"

"I don't know why."

"Well, if your son is so sure Miss Tillis is alive and has gone to Florida after her, why didn't he take her belongings?"

"It's Joel's responsibility to get her things. Why don't you ask her friends what happened to her belongings?"

Coach Davies contacted Tara for the scoop on what had gone on in Memphis and cautioned her. "You be careful. I know what I'm talking about. After Spicer died, I started getting strange telephone calls and odd things started happening to me."

Reporters converged on Northeast Louisiana University again. The press also swooped down on Joel's mother, ending her solitary agony—peaceful in comparison to straddling the high wires of the media circus erupting. Careful not to speculate or accuse Ivrin, she circumvented the stinging innuendoes: What did you expect? You knew he killed Brenda Spicer, yet helped him get off. Then you let your daughter live with him. Even now, you claim never seeing problems between them. Ideal fiancé, ideal couple.

She had to endure all the reporters. Though enemies, they were also allies in keeping police on the case. They demanded feeding, if only crumbs of insinuation. "Ivrin has a lot of explaining to do." A young reporter flinched: She sounded mildly annoyed, a schoolteacher scolding him for playing hooky. Joel's mother was also oddly hesitant to blast the Boldens for their outlandish statements to the press and swallowed her venom in silence.

Under media pressure, Memphis police conceded, "We feel there may be foul play. We've talked to Ivrin Bolden extensively and he sticks to his story. For now, we're treating this as a missing persons case. Sometimes they show up a little later. If she isn't found soon, we'll ask him to take polygraph tests."

Joel's mother suspected a stall and a call from Sergeant Donnor signaled the case was headed for the deep freeze, "I'm going on vacation. Keep your spirits up and I'll contact you when I get back." It was their last contact. When she telephoned Memphis, even the switchboard operator knew the Joel Tillis case by name. "No, Sergeant Donnor is working other cases. You'll have to speak with the officer in charge."

The days slugging by and the nights prowling, Joel's mother kept busy. The telephone and doorbell never stopped ringing. News coverage of the twist of events all referred to Spicer's murder two years before.

In Memphis, the case received two brief mentions in the newspaper. Without a smoking gun or a body, what local police were treating, at least to the public, as an episode of domestic violence made headlines in other places.

Joel's mother's imaginings of Joel sauntering into the kitchen explaining her absence collided with visions of Joel's cries for help from some distant place.

Chapter 48

Death's Smell

Six weeks later, near Forrest City, Arkansas, a hunter's dogs ran off. Whistling for them and wading through weeds, the hunter smelled death and turned his head, thinking to avoid an animal carcass nearby. Suddenly, something red caught his eye. It was partially covered by a sheet. The hunter pulled one edge of the sheet back and slapped at a swarm of green flies. The elements and predators had left a mutilated face and tennis shoes. A black brassiere was the only clue that the victim was a woman. Her skin had cracked and resembled rips in a tar paper shack, tissue had melted into puddles of rotted pink gelatin and what remained of her eyes ran as smeared mascara.

The hunter scrambled away from the horror and stench. To calm himself, he grabbed a beer from the cooler in his truck; then, he got in and sped to the sheriff's department.

Detective Bill Causey's prediction was accurate as radar—the dead woman was found twenty-five minutes from Memphis. Sheriff Dave Parkman searched law enforcement websites for cities or states with missing persons and found a possible match. A woman fitting the general description had disappeared from Memphis, their best shot based on proximity. Parkman felt sure she was in their morgue. As a result of the decomposition, preliminary reports guessed the victim to be much older than Joel Tillis— forty-five or fifty. But when Joel's sister heard white designer sneakers, she knew. Joel had worn them home for Mother's Day. Her gold watch was missing. An autopsy and dental records for a positive I.D. took four days.

Reporters spoke with Ivrin's father, "Knowing Joel, she's off sulking. They're hanging unfair publicity on that boy. Ivrin's pleasant, mannerly and smart like you won't find between here and Canada." Canada, Mexico and Argentina were a few of the speculations on his whereabouts.

Angered by his statements, Joel's mother lowered her guard. "We were waiting for the autopsy results. Ivrin's mother called me to gripe about the bad publicity they were putting on her baby."

A short while later, Joel's mother received confirmation. The dead woman *was* Joel Tillis and she had died of strangulation. Joel's mother made funeral arrangements and spoke with the press. "Some foul play has taken place here. I can't say what, where, why. But Ivrin was the last one to see her. Joel doesn't thumb rides. She isn't the type of girl who'd run away without telling us. For her to get that far without driving herself, something had to happen."

In the coffee room at the Monroe Police station, Detective Jim Gregory read Joel's mother's statement to other officers, "'Some foul play has taken place here.' Yeah, I'd go along with that. I had kind of ruled out suicide or natural causes myself."

Parkman and his deputy, Glenn Ramsey, reviewed files, "If he didn't do this one, too, a copy cat is biting his heels. He dumped her here to slow Memphis down."

Ivrin's father telephoned Joel's mother, who reported, "He asked how I was doing. I knew he was calling to find out the funeral details and cut him short."

Joel's sister grabbed the telephone and heard Ivrin's father say, "I've contacted my lawyer. We want another autopsy done to identify the body found in Arkansas."

The sister replied brokenly, "She's being buried tomorrow! Don't call here and upset my mother." She burst into tears and slammed the receiver down.

Joel's mother looked cosmopolitan in a champagne silk dress and side sweep hairdo. Her red eyes and face appeared tired, spontaneity snuffed out. Much she had known about Joel and Ivrin, but she hadn't known of obscene pictures or about Joel keeping a diary of her movements and a tell-all disk. What had she disclosed?

The private side of Joel's mother presided over the wake, replenishing platters of food and expressing her sadness to close relatives. The public side claimed she had suspected nothing amiss between Joel and Ivrin. Her daughter's murder was a mystery.

The segregated cemetery dated back to the 1800s: white citizens on the right, black citizens on the left, barring any mingling of ethnic spirits. The Baptist church, with its steeple peeling paint and stained glass paled by age, was a history book of social revolution and integrated for "Martha White's" memorial service.

Tributes were generous: "Joel had charm, extraordinary humor, an infectious laugh and passion for life."

"A dream was meeting Oprah Winfrey. Joel just knew she would make her co-host. A tomboy from birth, her tennis shoe laces were often untied, because she couldn't take the time."

A high school coach recalled her unselfishness. "It was never I, rather we and us. Never black and white, only people. Once she broke a team rule and I benched her. After the game, she gave me a Christmas gift as though she hadn't been reprimanded."

Cherise Gates, solemn and teary, wearing a pink moiré suit, pillbox hat and veil, was ushered to a front seat. *My mind vaulted back to her as an NLU journalism student sharing boisterous jokes about witnesses with Ivrin at his trial for Spicer's murder.*

Joel's long-time lover—such a fixture in her life—seemed both expected and unexpected. Church sisters dressed in white ushered mourners into pews. Quiet fell at twilight when Joel's portrait was placed on an easel: sitting on a bench overlooking Delta Bayou, smiling lazily and fancifully, seeing into some glorious future.

Joel would have loved the regal white casket with ornate gold handles. Her mother selected the Bible passage from Psalms: "Fret not thyself because of evildoers who prospereth in his way, for they shall be cut down like the grass…wither as the green herb…their sword enter into their own heart. The wicked in great power spreading themselves like a green bay tree shall be destroyed. Never envy the wicked. Trust in the Lord instead."

After the funeral, Memphis police were mystified by the overload of telephone calls about Joel Tillis. "Who was this woman, a movie star? Reporters from New Orleans to Stop Gap, Idaho, are blitzing us."

The media converged on Northeast Louisiana University. Best to push the broom in public rather than deny dirt in the house. A spokesman said, "It never went away, a black cloud hanging over us. It shows we don't know people as well as we think we do. That a second murder would come of this is mind-boggling."

Coach Davies commented, "Whether we were ahead ten points or behind by fifteen, Joel led the chants, cheered her teammates and motivated everybody. Through diligence, hard work and an explosion of energy, she made up for not having a great deal of talent. You don't expect things to hit so close to home."

Those who pegged Joel a survivalist spoke guardedly, "No need to judge the dead. She paid the ultimate dues."

Monroe detectives spotted the familiar gap of circumstantial evidence, "They have even less than we did. Bolden learned from us. Crossing the state line was a smart move."

In Forrest City, Parkman and Ramsey mulled it over. Physical evidence amounted to human hair and carpet fibers matching those in Joel's Memphis apartment—nothing else to prove she'd been murdered there, only the similarities between hers and the Spicer case, though witnesses now spoke out.

A difficult, expensive task with meager evidence to build a case, Memphis police seemed to some to see jurisdiction as Finders Keepers. By July their stance was clear, "Unless Sheriff Parkman is able to prove the victim was murdered here, the case is his to solve. Regardless, we'll support the agency conducting the investigation." Parkman told Ramsey, "I'm picking up whiffs of fertilizer from across the river. They're going to help us clear up their case. Mighty decent of them."

Causey prodded the Memphis police and he felt as though the attitude became, *Don't call us, we'll call you.*

Part 4

Southern Trail

Chapter 49

Fleeing

On the way to Florida, Ivrin dipped south to New Orleans and visited his best friend. Low on funds, he slept in his car several nights before renting an apartment in Hollywood, Florida, and a post office box—ready to move if Memphis or Arkansas came looking.

Miami was palm-tree perfect; faceless crowds, wealth and decadence, cops chasing aliens and drug runners, ideal for slipping through the Florida Keys and out of the country if necessary. In the melting pot metropolis, Ivrin Bolden could be Cuban, Puerto Rican or Jamaican.

Ivrin landed a job at a health laboratory and eager for romance again, he called a former classmate living in Miami. Aware of the murders, she promised to confirm their date and got an unlisted number.

In cooperation with Parkman, Shreveport police searched the Boldens' garage: "Jewelry but no personal papers. Computer boxed up. Suspect's mother said it belongs to her." Witnesses had told authorities about Joel's exposé disk, but in another snafu, the computer wasn't confiscated.

July and August passed with jurisdiction unsettled. Memphis police referred inquiries to their DA who refused calls from the media, outside law agencies and Joel's family. Professional courtesy spent, Parkman was irritated. The rank-and-file cooperated, but someone higher yanked the reins. In the media heat, the Memphis DA's office passed the hot skillet back to Forrest City and said tersely, "We're not pursuing him to Florida. He is not a suspect."

Parkman disagreed, "They have enough to bring him in again. He was developed as a suspect and they could have generated something from the information they had. It's frustrating. We put in a tremendous amount of time. Now the perpetrator's probably lying on a beach."

Without authority in Memphis and on a scant budget, Parkman couldn't justify a homicide that wasn't theirs and sent a memo to Memphis, "We are hand delivering all evidence to your office. Due to lack of proof a crime was committed here, we are closing the case."

A Memphis attorney spoke with me about his views on the shutdown. "We have a murder almost every day and a 95 percent clearance rate. The names Brenda Spicer, Joel Tillis and Ivrin Bolden don't mean zilch here and his parents have big bucks to fight any prosecution. Why go after a domestic case involving transients with a suspect who's fled the state?"

Joel's mother said, "My hands are tied by living in Louisiana. Ivrin consulted with a Memphis lawyer."

On the three-year anniversary of Brenda's murder, reporters interviewed the mother of Joel Tillis again and wondered if she caught the significance. "How are you able to handle this?"

"Through constant and fervent prayer. I don't let it eat at me. Naturally, I think about Joel. It's sad the way she went, but I had twenty-four good years with her. I believe in God's ability to see me through and justice in His own time." Alert to where the questions were leading, she steered away from any connection to Brenda's death.

Memphis conceded a dried-up case. "If we can't meet our burden of proof, regardless of the tragedy, we can't go forward. Though evidence points to Ivrin Bolden, we'd be stupid to go to court. Ted Bundy walked for a long time, too."

Joel's mother responded, "I'm beginning to think they're taking my daughter's death too lightly. I'm not understanding it and I can't get any answers. I've been taught to respect authority, to stand back and let them do their job."

Chapter 50

Lonely Cause

My impassioned cause was indeed a lonely one, dependent upon many dispassionate realists. How hard was it to accept that both murder cases were now closed and the killer was free?

In another television interview, Joel's mother said, "At the trial, I told what I knew as I remembered and believed it to be. After Joel died, I had my doubts, of course. It's just an unsolved mystery."

"With your own daughter's death, do you still think Ivrin Bolden was innocent of murdering Brenda Spicer?"

"I...had no reason to think differently...then." The spectre of her daughter's violent death loomed in the shadows, a lobo stalking her. Was the wolf freed from the trap so he could kill her daughter?

"I'm not accusing him, but I think he knows more than he's saying."

District Attorney Scott Taylor, stung by more criticism, hung the jury with culpability. "I knew our case was strong. The jury's decision should have been concern for another victim. I knew if he wasn't convicted, other people would die."

Judicial employees, law enforcement agents and trial followers asked the acid question, "I wonder what the jury has to say now." On the evening news, Joel's thick black hair and ruby jersey highlighting her paleness, the jury spokesperson said, "If Joel knew Ivrin was guilty, how could she have stayed with him? Now with this, it leads me to think someone covered up at the trial."

A Monroe policeman lobbed a magazine at his television set, "Noooo shit, Agatha Christie!"

A jury member said, "I feel a little bit guilty by letting him off. But he didn't look guilty."

"Not one of the murderers I've defended," said a local attorney, "had *Guilty* stamped on his or her forehead. The woman who poured lye on her three-month-old son while he slept wept like a Madonna in court."

Provoked jurors met with me. The only holdout for guilty said, "Since Ivrin claims his innocence then and now, he must be a very unlucky person to be accused twice. I'm revolted by the system, revolted that Joel Tillis died needlessly. My first jury duty will be my last."

Another juror claimed, "Eventually we'll have to go to professional juries. The system is getting too biased."

As he spoke, I thought of some witnesses—black, unbiased and courageous— who had withstood the pressures and contributed the most to the state's case.

"Defense Attorney Greer cinched it when he put up posters showing twelve areas of reasonable doubt. I'm sure the old man who held out for guilty feels right about it now. But the charge to the jury stressed the point of slightest doubt."

Another juror said, "We offered up many prayers for that little girl. She was looking for love and the lawyers blasted her in public. A lot was wrong about that trial."

Still another juror commented, "Bolden was a slick character. When Joel Tillis died the same way, I wanted to call defense lawyer Edwin Greer and ask him if he enjoyed his blood money. I felt so troubled, I couldn't sleep."

A female juror also spoke of intense internal pressures, "Going in, another juror was convinced of Bolden's guilt. A female juror devoted herself to changing his mind. Her charm played a big role in the outcome."

Though one juror had kept belief in humanity even after being beaten, robbed and her house set afire, she lost faith in the courts: "I have strong opinions about that trial and none of them are good."

Six jurors, with the initial split verdict still fresh in their minds, said they had never felt unanimous, even after being badgered to acquit. The foreperson remembered it differently. "I and the majority of the jurors, almost to being unanimous, believed absolutely in Ivrin's innocence. We wondered how the case could have been brought to court. The police, attorneys, coaches and friends of Joel and Brenda knew so much that wasn't presented to us. I realize now that the DA and witnesses concealed a lot. I was naive about fatal attractions and Joel and Ivrin's relationship."

She commented, "I'll never understand my bell-clear premonition that I would be chosen, that some universal force at work meant for me to sit on that jury."

How could she not have admired Defense Attorney Greer's phenomenal recall of any detail favoring his client? "He organized and presented his case as the only reasonable conclusion. Miss Devreaux was bright and committed, but hampered by inexperience."

The foreperson cried. "When Joel died, the shock hit me, then indescribable pain. The trial came back in a rolling action of being physically lifted into waves of grief. So many flashbacks torment me. I see how nervous Joel was on the stand and I now recognize her hostility. She never looked at Ivrin, which was unnatural. I chalked it up to righteous indignation. What reason did she have to lie? That weak line of wanting a rich husband didn't fly. If the state had made a case of what was being held over her head, we might have doubted her."

A Lady Indian asked another teammate, "If we could rewind the clock back to Spicer and know he would murder Joel, too, if convicting him and saving her meant revealing your darkest secret in court, would you do it now?"

Her roommate studied the campus below the dorm window. Lovers raced by in sporty cars, tanned young men jogged as girls sitting on the grass pretended not to notice. In a voice thick with melancholy, she replied, "No. Would you?"

As Joel had, they knew the rules. They might drown trying to save someone, donate a kidney or protest intolerance. But enduring self-immolation, being branded as deviant and made the brunt of jokes and contempt was unbearable.

Discontentment with the status quo pervaded Monroe. Taylor and his supporters expressed confidence that this September election against two opponents wouldn't be much of a race. They attacked, "He isn't a trial lawyer, provides no leadership to his staff." Parading the Spicer and Tillis murders in speeches to civic clubs, Taylor's rivals voiced their views. It appeared to many that his office botched the case. An opponent's television advertisement showed the victory photo of Ivrin and Joel with the headline, "Bolden Acquitted."

Taylor barely slid into a runoff and lost.

Even in Italy and Spain, former Lady Indians playing the professional circuits fielded remarks from competitors, "So you're from the lesbian university where those murders happened?"

A Northeast Louisiana University professor said, "I thought of contacting *60 Minutes* or *20-20* to press for pursuit of the case, but decided I had to do it myself." The "let-Diane-Sawyer-do-it" mentality was widespread. Critical of the judicial system, the matter was consigned to platitudes that the guilty are always punished.

After leaving the DA's office with plans to move out of state, Emily Devreaux got married. In seclusion, with an unlisted phone number and five months pregnant, she agreed to meet with me.

Her defeat and the censures flooded back. She felt sorry for Joel, whom she could have liked under different circumstances. "I don't believe Edwin Greer will take the case this time around." *I disagreed—Greer was professional to the core and he remained a consultant to the Boldens. Devreaux now had a life outside of law books. The Bolden case was her first and last criminal trial.*

Chapter 51

Frustrating Journey

I resumed the frustrating journey. Some believed the murders of Brenda Spicer and Joel Tillis would've been best forgotten. Yet the public, the Monroe police who had given their best and insiders guided by conscience wanted the true story revealed. The principled emerged from the shadows to tell what they knew.

Access to public records was often a war of salesmanship, appointments were broken, interviews declined or fruitless as witnesses filtered their words. The D. A.'s chief investigator, who had also served under Taylor, attempted to rewrite my book, "You're a nice lady. I know you'll be careful not to hurt or embarrass anyone. No one's to blame but the perpetrator."

When Taylor's secretary gave me the Spicer case files to research, she inadvertently gave me a red file folder of the grand jury testimony. Leaving and then coming back to the law library to check on me, she noticed and rushed to retrieve it.

In Arkansas, Sheriff Parkman kept the Tillis murder file in his desk. With the cases technically closed, he let me visit and research his records. Cordial and open, he toured me around town and took me to lunch.

Memphis authorities responded tersely, "We can't meet with you. This is a very controversial case." *They're telling me?*

Detective Ken Carson agreed to see me in exchange for anonymity and my promise not to ask for specific details. I didn't say I'd spent the last two days in Arkansas accessing their reports. "Everything's busted loose at work," he said. "I'm working late, so call me around 4:00. We're cleaning up another one of your cases from Louisiana." *You haven't cleaned up the first one, I thought.*

I called him as arranged. "Detective Carson has already gone for the day." *When he wasn't there, I dialed his pager. Some of the characters waiting to use the phone in the restroom hallway made paging a cop seem like a smart idea. A half-hour passed. Locating my motel in a strange city in rush hour traffic, I thought, What am I doing here? Back at my motel room, I paged Carson again and he responded.*

At a restaurant—noisy with less opportunity to ask compromising questions—Carson folded his arms on his chest, eyeing me.

I brought up Joel Tillis's murder. "Departmental policy restrains me from voicing my opinions about the case. Mr. Bolden is taking an extended vacation. One day we'll bring him home to Memphis."

The azaleas and crepe myrtles bloomed pink and watermelon along the Ouachita river; snowy dogwoods banked the hills in the season of resurrection. A rebirth of faith did not come. Two jurors from the Brenda Spicer trial attended a culinary school and by accident sat across from each other. The troubling trial lingered as an unfinished quarrel. "We got in too big a hurry on that case. We didn't take enough time."

The former foreperson asked, "Oh? And what if we had taken more time, would it have made any difference?"

"I think so. It would make a difference in how I feel."

Although my search for the truth kept hitting problems, I felt a vague peace for trying to quiet the spirits of the two women betrayed by the system. And I was not about to give up.

Next I tried to reach Lady Indian Wendy Ballard, who cancelled our appointment. "Coach Davies called a meeting and threatened to yank our scholarships over this."

Obviously, it preyed on Davies's mind. If the story must be told she wanted it told her way: Doris Davies versus the NCAA and NLU. She told several players, "I was approached by a former professor. He wanted to collaborate about my coaching years, the championship, the NCAA probation and Spicer's murder. I turned him down. After Joel died, he contacted me again and I'm giving it some thought."

As another season ended, Davies—blamed and under NLU's eagle eye— seemed to buckle. Parents complained of mood swings and doldrums about sign- ing new talent and winning. The long downer had doused her competitive edge.

Kim Cameron said, "We were winning a game with a good edge. Davies argued with the referee, got a technicality and we lost."

Doris Davies had enough years in education to retire and left without even a press conference. Wendy said, "The university pretended to be surprised at her retirement, but announcements to the team that Davies was out and Coach Anderson was in came down boom-boom."

Someone had to take the long overdue fall. Accolades of Davies's sixteen years at Northeast Louisiana University were oddly rationed. "She did a fine job as women's basketball coach. We appreciate all the good things she's done." *Sans a banquet or testimonial, the NLU president was noticeably silent.*

I set up a lunch meeting with Joel's mother. "Can my daughter who looks after me now join us?"

Cordial and personable, Joel's mother disarmed me as she had some at Ivrin's trial. She conceded a little bitterness, "He didn't call to let me know about Joel." *Not that she thought he did it—an etiquette faux pas, I thought.*

She brushed off my theory about a pattern, the possibility that other women might die. To her, only her daughter was germane. Expressions hardened when I mentioned Brenda's murder and a return to motive. Joel's sister theorized about other possible suspects. Their concern was nailing Ivrin without digging up the first ghost. "About Brenda's death, I heard the police questioned a top NLU administrator's son."

"That was a baseless rumor the police thought was hatched and spread as a diversionary tactic." I paid the lunch ticket. The three of us glanced at each other. I had seen the look often: How do you think it went?

The next morning, instinct—that Internal Voice or Psychic Shove that had pushed me forward throughout this search for the truth—directed me to the Greenlawn Cemetery. I searched the row where I remembered Joel's gravesite to be, but I couldn't find it by reading tombstones and almost gave up. Finally, by comparing the lustre of silver paint on the masonry used to seal the above ground vaults, I distinguished newer graves from older ones. The only marker, barely readable after a year in the elements, was the small sticker funeral homes use to tag graves.

Chapter 52

Ominous Visitor

After a brutal massacre of several co-eds in Florida, which Ivrin had nothing to do with, conjectures ran wild in Monroe. Noting similarities to the Spicer and Tillis cases, a law enforcement officer called the tip line and investigators brought Ivrin in for questioning, dousing his hopes that authorities had forgotten him.

Ivrin's supervisor wrote on his termination, "He didn't show up or call in for two days. No one knew where he was."

After his alibi in Miami checked out, Ivrin moved from Florida. En route to Shreveport to see his family, he traveled through Monroe on Interstate 20. My research confirmed the timing.

I lived in the parish two miles off the interstate. Fate would have its way again. I happened to be reading on the side patio when a car slowed to a crawl and stopped in front of my home. The driver clasped his hands on the steering wheel and stared. I looked into the face of Ivrin Bolden. Not since the trial had I imagined seeing him, nor would I imagine it again. Someone must have tipped him off that I was researching the cases. If I hadn't been outside, would he have knocked on my door?

Strangely, I wasn't terrified. As I reflected on his appearance at my home, I comprehended the miscalculations of his victims: the world is a lulling cradle, our surroundings so ordinary and we all live forever. However, since I felt less safe, I had a security alarm system complete with bells, sirens and ominous warnings installed.

Soon I learned that with a new social security number, Ivrin reapplied for an Army commission and was accepted into six-month training at Fort Lee, Virginia.

Part 5

Delran

Chapter 53

New
Flames

At Fort Lee, an acquaintance invited Ivrin for a weekend to meet her parents and sister. "I want to show you New Jersey—beautiful forests, gardens and lakes, close to Atlantic City and the Big Apple."

He felt an immediate Henry Higgins-Eliza Doolittle attraction to his friend's younger sister, Michelle Peterson. She was young, pretty and impressionable, eager to be molded by their charming visitor. Again, it appeared as though acceptance into her family was as important as being with her and Ivrin would say with pride, "I stayed with Michelle's family on furloughs and they included me in their social events and special occasions."

The home of Ivrin's new girlfriend was as noisy and casual as Joel's mother's had been. Ivrin talked of going back to school to impress; he repeated the pattern of courting both daughter and mother. Michelle's mother became Ivrin's new one.

Burlington County, New Jersey, rooted in Colonial history, dates back to the Lenni-Lanape Indians when Englishmen, lured by beauty and plenty, settled the land before William Penn mapped out Philadelphia across the river. Nudging the vanishing truck farms, notables seeking haven from urban cities built millionaire estates.

Puritan ethics held in the blink-and-you-miss-it hamlets. On a maple-shaded street in Mount Holly, the Old Courthouse built in 1796 and preserved as a fine example of Early American wooden architecture harmonized with the neighborhood: a charmingly skinny structure where tourists imagined Colonial Dames sipping tea in Victorian lace. Any resemblance to Cobblestone Lane and simpler times was deceiving.

Next door, County Prosecutor Stephen Raymond ran an innovative operation noted for building cases solid as Plymouth Rock. Detective Annette Trivelli of the Sex Crimes Unit was a fierce proponent for victims dead or alive.

After Ivrin graduated, he didn't get his Army commission and they discharged him. The past had caught up with him. As the holdout juror in Monroe had foreseen, "He'll be running all of his life."

Ivrin told Michelle, "They couldn't get my papers straight. I'm moving to New Jersey to be near you." Ivrin needed her fawning adoration and landed two jobs: in the laboratory of a milk processing plant and, astoundingly, as a part-time counselor to emotionally troubled youth at a state boys' school. He found satisfaction as a role model again, befriending borderline children scarred, abused or wayward. After being harrassed by cops in three states, he understood the abuse life dumped on victims.

In his spare time, he acted like Pygmalion trying to transform the pliant Michelle by teaching her to write a résumé, to dress appropriately for job interviews and project self-confidence. Her parents were awed.

By September, they lived together. He called Michelle's mother almost daily just to chat and boasted to a co-worker, "I have a wonderful connection with Michelle's family, especially with her mother, because of my positive influence on her. I've established her in finding work and I'm paying her bills."

Early on, he had pegged her very insecure. Boyfriends before him had dated others and she was suspicious of any contact he had with other women.

When Ivrin's car started breaking down and showing its mileage, Michelle's sister accepted his offer to buy her newer model before she left for overseas duty. He would pay the notes and insurance and they could transfer the title on her return to the States.

He gave in to Michelle's incessant curiosity by confiding in her to a degree, "I was always pressured to come in first at everything. Good wasn't good enough. That's why I work so hard and press you to improve."

She sensed Ivrin hid their love affair by calling his mother from work. Maybe he was ashamed of their living together and didn't want his family to know about her. The catch of a lifetime, she wanted to share his innermost thoughts, marry him and have his babies, but he gave no sign of introducing her to his family. Michelle rehashed the puzzle of what mystery surrounded his past life. In late October after he left for work, she played sleuth and in a book of his, inside a drawer, she found a news clipping about Brenda Spicer. She showed it to him as soon as he came home. "We have to talk. I need to know about this."

He insisted, "I didn't do it. I was found innocent." She hugged him around the waist. "I know you're too nice to do anything like that."

About Joel, his former girlfriend whose death was highlighted in the article, Ivrin said, "We argued a lot, broke up because of financial problems and went our separate ways."

On the surface, they dropped the subject, but Michelle's snooping consumed him. Did he feel she was another bitch messing with his head to make him a puppet? Why did women pry through every cranny to manipulate him?

"We even talked about marriage," she told her family. "Not naming a date, but considering it." Nevertheless, it was clear he had misgivings. Her clinging ways and contentment to work as a cook bored him. Joel had evaded him as quicksilver. Michelle was Play-Doh, malleable yet messy, no easy way to get rid of her.

An older co-worker, Victoria, was Ivrin's intellectual equal and a sympathetic listener, describing him as, "Professional and well-liked, a good all-around person. He became my little brother and talked of the high expectations of his family and their friends, of not being allowed to fail at anything and of being pushed beyond his limits. He loved his sister, but I detected a little jealousy. She got a new car in high school, but he had to work and get his own." The hard luck story was slanted.

When Victoria invited him to Thanksgiving dinner, Michelle felt deserted. He fit in with Victoria's family, gorging on turkey and trimmings, laughing, joking and watching the parades on television.

In December, his family planned a visit and he told Michelle, "I need you to stay with your parents while they're here." Devastated, she pressed him, "Why are you afraid for me to meet them?" Did it have to do with the article and why would his parents object to their romance?

As Joel had said, "Everything changed after Brenda's murder." And everything had changed when Michelle found the news clipping. Arguing over his secrecy and friendships with women at work, she threatened to leave in her sister's car. Déjà vu, Joel leaving him stranded. Later she commented that coming off his rage, he said, "If you'd taken off and I had caught you, I'd have killed you." Though shocked, she probably rationalized that Joel walking out had left him wary of feeling abandoned. But was another paramount issue her behaving as though his car still belonged to her sister?

To a man already upset by a tumultuous past with two women, would it be surprising if he labeled his new girlfriend probing? With her knowledge of his legal problems, was he feeling he wanted to lose her?

He told Victoria, "I see characteristics I don't respect and I don't want to live with her anymore. I'm taking her home to her mother's while I think about things." Michelle scorned that it might be dangerous; rather than throw her out he had to ease her out.

"His feelings for me flip-flopped overnight," she told her family. "It's weird. He told me to leave for a cooling off period, but don't take all my things, hinting he might take me back." Extending a carrot that their split was temporary, he fed her hope.

"Why won't you let me stay? What's wrong?'" Michelle asked.

"I'm at a violent point of doing something bad and I promised myself I wouldn't hurt you. I have a bad temper. Take what clothes you need. I need space to chill out." He denied another woman was in the picture.

In January, Ivrin invited Michelle to lunch and drove her to a gun shop. "I've found a gun I want you to see." Though she was delighted to be with him again, Michelle asked, "Why do you need a gun?"

"For protection. It's all legal; I'm applying for a permit to carry it." It didn't scare her. Ivrin refused to see her. She still had a key, came over, cooked gourmet meals and left them on the stove. According to his interrogation with police, he kept thinking she would hook up with another guy.

First Brenda was murdered in 1987, then Joel in 1989. Spring and the deadly anniversaries beckoned.

Chapter 54

Fierce Forebodings

At the yellow cinder block building of the Delran Police Department, Ivrin applied for a handgun permit. He listed Michelle's mother as a reference, which reflected sardonic megalomania. On "Previous Addresses," he omitted Monroe, Memphis, Miami and his Army stint at Fort Lee.

Under "Reason for wanting gun," he wrote, "Constitutional Right." To the questions, "Have you ever been convicted of a crime that was not expunged or sealed? Been arrested in another state? Received treatment for a mental illness?" He checked "No" to all. In New Jersey, applicants were actually charged with falsifying information. He must have gambled on obscuring the past.

Detective Ed Perrino, who screened applications, expected the typical dull reading. Usual responses to "Reason For Wanting A Gun" were self-protection, husband works night shift or bad neighborhood. Constitutional Right. Perrino patted the form; it had a bit of an arrogant, what's-it-to-you attitude. He surmised two things: Ivrin Bolden disliked cops and had a chip on his shoulder.

Nineteen years on the force gave Perrino a healthy paranoia. He marked the application for routine check through National Crime Information and the Spicer case bingoed back. Joel's death didn't show up since Memphis had never arrested or charged Ivrin.

Perrino telephoned the Monroe Police Department. Almost expected, Causey's nemesis was coming around again. Causey said, "We know he killed Brenda Spicer. And he killed his girlfriend, Joel Tillis, in Memphis. They had even less evidence than we did. He dates women he can control and is very possessive. His profile shows he hates women and will do it again."

"I need a copy of your file. We're keeping an eye on him. The thought of him counseling young boys and the prospect of him buying a gun here gives me the willies." Without legal basis for denial, they could only delay.

Perrino contacted Annette Trivelli at the D. A.'s office. "I'm concerned. He's definitely a suspect in the second murder in Memphis. Jurisdictional matters interfered and the case is still open. Lewd photos surfaced in Memphis's probe. I'm concerned about him working at the state boys' school."

Trivelli bounced it off Detective Michael "Mickey" King who said, "Unless Memphis charges him or he commits a crime here, all we can do is stall." The permit delay interrupted Ivrin's schedule and played on his nerves. Questions must have surfaced in Ivrin's mind, like if the cops were tailing him, had they tapped his phone or had Michelle already talked?

Soon, Ivrin met Carolyn Buchner, a young and pretty co-worker, educated and self-possessed. Ivrin took her out four nights straight and may have asked himself if she could aid his plan. Why would he ice Michelle when he and Carolyn were a hot item?

On Valentine's Day, he ordered his standard red roses: a dozen for Carolyn and a dozen for her mother. Michelle was on a fact-finding mission in his apartment and found the invoice. She called the florist who notified Ivrin, "Some woman is trying to find out who you ordered flowers for."

Ivrin had never dealt with a woman who clung so hard, but he needed the good graces of the Peterson family. Otherwise, they might screw him out of his payments on the sister's car and Michelle might blab. He paid the Petersons a friendly visit and when Michelle walked him to the car, she spotted a greeting card from Carolyn over his visor. She flew into a rage and ripped it. Then she showed up at his work furious to check Carolyn out and scared the girls in the office. Ivrin warned her she was trespassing on private property.

She called Carolyn, "I'm Ivrin's fiancée. You and I need to meet and talk. Ivrin and I are going through a thing, but are getting back together soon."

Ivrin assured Carolyn, "I broke up with her weeks ago, but she's hell-bent on wrecking my job and my life. She's a nut. The day I asked her to leave, she lost her job. Without a job, she's devoted full-time to checking up on me."

Michelle knew about his implication in Brenda's murder for months and had done nothing. He was in control. "I want you to come get all your things," he told her over the phone.

According to Michelle, when she arrived, Ivrin sat on the sofa lacing a pair of new shoes. Ivrin pulled the laces tight and yanked the bows saying, "Remember that article? Well, I did it. I also killed Joel. I strangled both of them." She felt the prospect that she could be next throbbing in the room— too foreboding for even her to miss.

Later, she reported that the room felt chilly and darkness had fallen outside. She eased to the door with her hand on the knob. "If you strangled them, why aren't you in prison?"

"They didn't have enough evidence, babe. I covered my tracks. I don't want you to tell anybody, okay?"

She fished her car keys from her purse.

"The Memphis cops stayed on my back. I moved to Florida, then here. So you see why we have to split. I want your promise you're not going to tell anybody."

"Yes, I promise but you're lying. The real reason is Carolyn." Icy wind stung her cheeks as she ran to her mother's car.

In the kitchen, Michelle's mother ladled spaghetti sauce. "Ivrin told me he's killed two women. I found a news article about it back in October. He says he did it."

"That's absurd. Ivrin isn't the type to harm anybody. He's just upset about your bust-up."

"No Mama, he meant it. He made me promise not to say anything."

"This whole mess is out of hand. Stay away from him."

Michelle wavered. It could be his way of dumping her, she probably thought. She had copied the work number of Ivrin's mother off his résumé and called to introduce herself. "That's crazy. Ivrin didn't kill anyone. He's probably under stress from working so hard and needs some time alone. Do what he asks and leave."

"But he said he killed his girlfriend in Memphis."

Ivrin's mother wasted no time in warning her son about his pattern of getting involved with what she may have viewed as another devious woman and laying himself open to more ruin.

Later, it was reported that Michelle dialed the women's shoe store in Memphis where Joel Tillis had worked, another number she'd lifted from his papers. A new employee said, "We don't have a Joel Tillis working here." Maybe she had gotten married or really was dead. "It blew my mind," she told her sister. "He said he did it but his mother said he didn't. He phoned me and said, 'You promised not to tell. Then you call my mother.'"

"I also called Memphis."

"All I want you to do is leave me alone."

Michelle's anger simmered and Carolyn noticed her hanging around the parking lot in front of the apartment building.

Chapter 55

Chilled

I *learned through a police source that Ivrin was in New Jersey and had applied for the gun permit. I also found out that a persistent Italian cop was watching him closely. It filtered down that when Detective Ed Perrino first called Bill Causey, he had shared the titillating bulletin with church friends who had known Brenda and Joel.* "I wanted you to know where he is, but keep it quiet."

Causey's attitude toward me had chilled. I felt he thought I was a meddler. I phoned him at the station, "Just wondering if you'd heard anything about where Bolden is?"

"He's still in Florida." *He was humoring a pesky gadfly.*

"Any new developments in Memphis on Tillis's case?"

"No, haven't heard anything."

Before he left for work, Ivrin received a hang-up call he assumed was from Michelle. She recruited a male friend with a van. Ivrin had placed a lockout order with the apartment manager which barred her from the premises. The security guard said she showed her driver's license with photo identification and her parents' address, "I used to live here, but I've lost my key and I need to move some things. I'm trying to avoid any bad scenes with my ex-boyfriend." He agreed to let her in if she signed the standard forms as a former resident there to remove her belongings.

Carolyn came home to a ransacked apartment—contents of the bedroom were scattered on the floor, pot plants unearthed on the carpet and the remaining television set was broken and lying on its side. She raced to a pay phone and Ivrin sped home. The cops were jacking him around about a gun; if they wouldn't let him protect himself, it was their job to do it. If Michelle didn't return what she'd stolen, he'd have her arrested and if she flapped her mouth, who would believe a burglar? The world operated on leverage. She would keep the secrets or cool her tail in jail, he probably thought. Memphis wasn't after him anymore and he was guilty of nothing in New Jersey.

His complaint to the Delran police read: "Doors were locked, indicating person had a key. Victim stated all items stolen were bought prior to his involvement with the accused and not community property." The security guard stated that Michelle and a male had gained entry. An arrest warrant was issued for burglary and theft, with a summons to appear in court on charges of criminal mischief.

According to later statements, he phoned Michelle's mother and said, "Your daughter stole all my things and destroyed everything in my apartment."

"What are you talking about? No! She wouldn't do that."

"She did. There's a warrant for her arrest and I'm getting a search warrant for your house. All I want is my stuff back."

March 13 was my birthday. Eleven hundred miles away, two police officers had arrested Michelle Peterson. "Suspect was read Miranda. Admitted going into apartment to pick up two gold rings. Denied taking other items. Released on $500 bail."

Perrino squinted at the burglary report and hummed a favorite song. The complainant was the "Constitutional Rights" guy. Shake it up and see what falls out.

Chapter 56

Opening Old Wounds

New Jersey's domestic violence laws place the burden on the accused with mandatory arrest before proven guilty. Perrino told Michelle, "Along with theft and criminal mischief charges, Mr. Bolden also filed a restraining order preventing you from returning to the scene or any further contact with him." While he legally kicked her butt, he still had illegal possession of her sister's car.

Ivrin was surprised when Michelle's mother went to his job and demanded the car keys. "Why are you reneging? I've paid the notes and I have an agreement. If I get my stuff back, this'll go away."

"There's a whole bed of snakes under that charm you lay on people, Ivrin."

At the police department, Michelle talked before she hit the chair in Perrino's office. "Let me tell you about this guy. I found a clipping where he was charged and acquitted of murdering a girl in Louisiana. He came right out and admitted, 'Yeah, I've strangled two women and I can do it again.'

He didn't act worried about me knowing."

"Would you talk to the county prosecutor?" Perrino pressed.

"I'll talk to anybody."

For input on applying the squeeze, Perrino called Causey. "Bolden's as busy as a cranberry picker. Another girlfriend, now his ex, had been living with him. He kicked her out and she returned to his apartment to get what she thought she was due and trashed the place. He's charged her with theft and criminal mischief. Here's the biggie—she claims he admitted doing your girl in Monroe and the one in Memphis."

"He's finally coughed it up," Causey replied.

"I've sent it to the county prosecutor. Since your case is dead, it'll take Forrest City or Memphis to flip the switch. Up here, he's clean. You think they want us to run with it?"

"I prodded Memphis to pursue it. They told me not to call back, that it wouldn't be prosecuted. Sheriff Parkman in Arkansas is the catalyst. The ex-girlfriend had better run. I'd tell her to leave town, change her name and don't leave any tracks."

Burlington County wasn't as laid-back. They had a 100 percent clearance rate for the past eight years, with most cases in cooperation with outside agencies. A jurisdictional dumping ground, the truism was, "Those whacked in Philadelphia wash ashore in New Jersey." Ivrin had stumbled into a mythical Lake Woebegone of law enforcement.

Prosecutor Stephen Raymond, Assistant Prosecutor Rocky Minervino and Detectives Scott Fitz-Patrick and Michael King brainstormed the case. "What do you think? In his own words, Ivrin told Peterson he's feeling violent, ready to do something bad. He's under pressure and blowing up."

Raymond said, "He's up to his earlobes in girlfriends. Still, we need to put it together fast. The only way to prevent him buying a gun and get him off our streets is to shoulder the load for Memphis and Arkansas."

King responded, "It isn't as though we don't have enough work of our own. Memphis's shorts aren't in a wad. Why should we bust it for them?"

Fitz-Patrick said, "Sheriff Parkman is eager to cooperate and wants us to interview Michelle Peterson."

The detectives were bewildered by Memphis's cool response. "If all they need is evidence, they should be whistling Dixie and twirling a fire baton."

"Southern inscrutability, talk slow, walk slow, react slow."

Their office motto was, *Remove the "I" to widen your vision. We is the key. Team Work with Independent Thinking. Work smart, not hard.* Yellow-sticky reminders on a bulletin board read: "*Intuition—the immediate knowing of something, unencumbered by the process of thought.*"

"We need to wire Peterson. Bolden's already tried to lure her back over there. Going face-to-face could endanger her. If she calls him at home, he won't say much in front of his new girlfriend. At work, he may get rattled and make a slip."

"Just go easy," Fitz-Patrick told her. "Keep him on the line as long as you can. You're calling to negotiate with him about the charges and your court date on the restraining order."

The telephone receptionist told her, "Sorry, he's out in the plant and unavailable at this time."

"It's an emergency. Tell him Michelle needs to talk to him."

Ivrin alerted the receptionist not to accept her calls, but it would give him more ammunition when they went to court. "Ivrin, I found out that Joel is dead. I called Memphis."

"Uh-huh, uh-huh." He sounded impatient, wary of talking on the phone as if smelling the odor of cops.

"So you did kill Joel, huh?"

"No. I didn't kill anybody, sweetheart."

"But you told me you did. And I know that she's dead."

"So why are you telling me this?"

"Because I have a subpoena to court on Thursday. If you don't drop the charges, I can always tell the police."

"I haven't done anything. I'm sure the cops already know all about this. It's no big secret where I am if Memphis wants me."

"I figure we can negotiate something."

"All you have to do is return what you stole."

Polygraphist Bob Scara analyzed the tape. "Angry, jittery, a bit haughty, a degree of admission in the statement, 'I'm sure the cops already know all about this. It's no big secret where I am if Memphis wants me.' He must have told her he killed the two girls. Otherwise he would have been shocked when she brought it up." The police felt they could time a reaction from him with a stopwatch.

Perhaps afraid that the problems would affect his love nest, he told Carolyn, "Michelle called me at work. I'm filing another complaint."

"What did she say?"

"Oh, she was nice. But she tried to blackmail me into dropping the charges. Hey, I'm wiped. Let's go to bed."

"Blackmail you over what?"

"Just something that happened in the past. I really don't want to talk about it." He turned over and went to sleep.

The next morning Ivrin met with Detective Perrino. "Since she's still harassing you, we need to bump this up to the county and get a stronger restraining order. Why don't I make an appointment? You can give them the details and they'll go from there."

He agreed. It only had to do with what he may have viewed as the loony bimbo stealing his things and trying to blackmail him. She was in a lot more trouble than he was. If she squawked, he would have explained his side first.

Fitz-Patrick and King psyched up with the Rules of The Mission: *Stay out of the GRIP. Professional, unemotional, bring no baggage into the interview. Be objective. Don't offend. Positive approach, avoid the negative. Get the subject to talk. Listen more, talk less. Detect deception and obtain the truth.*

Fitz-Patrick was a clean-cut professional in leading criminals to catharsis. He shook hands with Ivrin and he introduced Annette Trivelli, "She works domestic violence cases." To Ivrin, she must have seemed to be in her early twenties, reticent, a pert little social worker wearing a beige suit. In reality, she was thirty-one, tenacious and perceptive to assess any cracks in his mask.

"This is a serious matter we want to assist you with," said Fitz-Patrick. "Would you give a formal statement to determine the facts surrounding her violating the restraining order?"

"No problem," Ivrin said.

"First, why are you filing this complaint?"

"She called me to try and get the burglary charges dropped. After our breakup and before the burglary, she kept calling, even came to my job. I was dating another girl. Michelle wouldn't leave me alone and violated the restraining order again last night by calling my work."

They seemed sympathetic and Ivrin appeared to warm to the role of beleaguered lover and model citizen. Fitz-Patrick and Trivelli respected his rights and saw he was too good for his own good.

Fitz-Patrick noted: Subject didn't volunteer Peterson had confronted him with admissions made earlier regarding Tillis's death. Only after detailed questioning did he mention it.

"What made her think she could get you to drop the charges?"

"She knows in my past I was indicted on second degree murder in Louisiana and found not guilty and is trying to use that as bribery...that she'd release information to the police.

"I told her everything was cleared. I'm not under a rock somewhere. The police departments probably know where I am."

"What reason did she give you to drop the charges?"

"She didn't want to go through getting a lawyer and going to court. I told her, you know, I'm the victim of a criminal act, just seeking my compensation and wherever the court system would follow, that's where I'm going with it."

"So there was sort of a quid pro quo agreement she was trying to get you to enter into that if you would drop your case, she wouldn't reveal information about you?"

"Right."

"And that's important. In what tenor did Miss Peterson present that to you?"

"That she'd dug into my background and found out more information she'd reveal to cause me any type of character problems to discredit me in the community. I told her I wasn't going to fall for that, because my character speaks for itself."

"Did she mention money? Compensation?"

"No."

He talked about her fatal attraction. She did everything but leave a pet rabbit simmering in his stew pot. "She continued to check up on me and harass me and Carolyn."

"What information was she trying to use against you?"

"She had found a news article about me in one of my books."

"Now, what led her to use that as a form of bribery or defamation of character to threaten you with?" the detectives asked.

"That's what's baffling me. This is information known throughout our relationship. If she felt in any danger living with me, why didn't she leave? She knows my character in the community is very positive because of my personality. I take great care to portray that around people. Stay upbeat and happy. So that would be a point where she could attack me with bribery. Before this incident, I had wonderful ties with her family, especially her mother, because of my good influence on Michelle." *Quite the choirboy*, Trivelli probably thought, *reputation means everything.*

He was spilling over like Niagara Falls and they let him pour. "After I broke up with her, she called my mother asking questions about the trial in Louisiana. I didn't want my mother worrying about the incidents going on up here and I had already been through one legal altercation that caused me not to complete medical school. I was upset. In January, I explained I had grown away from her and I didn't want us to end up in a bad disagreement. I wanted to stay friends with her and her family. When she found out about Carolyn, she went nuts. So I asked her to move all her things out and leave the keys."

Fitz-Patrick nodded, "Now Miss Peterson claims she found an article about the trial in Louisiana and it mentioned a girlfriend named Joel...a Joel Tillis? Now where is she living?"

"Joel and I were engaged. It was her best friend that the trial in Louisiana was based on. I don't know if any charges were ever brought against anyone in Memphis. I lost my job because I didn't go to work when I found out Joel was missing. Then I moved from Memphis."

Ivrin's nose appeared to itch and they watched him rub it. Research indicates the nostrils flare during deception and to a suspect feel the size of a puff adder snake; he or she will often try to contain the inflation by rubbing them. "Michelle did some snooping by calling Memphis about the whereabouts of Joel Tillis and was threatening me with letting that information out to the police here and to the public. She learned my last girlfriend was found dead, that I'd been questioned and the case closed. She was threatening to say I might have had something to do with Joel Tillis's death. I thought she'd move on and date other men. The time she's put into trying to break up me and Carolyn is shocking me to death."

"Yeah, it seems she's gone to great length to malign you."

"Right. Do all she can to cause damage to me."

"And what was the name of the girl in Louisiana?"

"Oh God, what was it? Brenda...I think...Brenda Spicer." Crossing his legs, he rubbed his nose again.

"So Joel Tillis is separate from that case?"

"Yes."

"Now what eventually happened with that?"

"After Joel left, I called around trying to locate her, because I didn't want her mother to worry. I asked her if another guy Joel had taken home with her to Hammond knew anything. After Joel was found dead, I flew back to Memphis from Florida to give another statement."

"As for Michelle Peterson trying to use that as a blackmail ploy, were you considered a suspect in Memphis in Joel Tillis's death?"

"I think I was at that...when...I think after they found her body, I was considered a suspect."

"And why was that?"

"Well, we had argued that morning and they claimed I was the last person who saw her."

"So you told them of the other boyfriend Joel had?"

"Uh-huh. And I asked my family to check on Joel's family to see if they needed anything. I didn't contact her mother myself because she'd gone through a traumatic time. But if they needed any other information, I'd help them out as much as I could."

The statement had taken four hours. "Oh wow," Ivrin said, relieved and ready to go.

"We'll review the transcript and contact you about the restraining order violation."

They called Sheriff Parkman with the breakthrough, "We need a hard shove from your direction for grounds to pursue it."

"I'll try to build a fire under Memphis."

The prosecutors viewed Ivrin Bolden as a complex suspect who lied and manipulated to avoid arrest, had an unlisted phone number and had fled north to outrun his past. Yet he called attention to himself. His confession to Michelle and his own statement to them seemed like a man flaunting invincibility while craving punishment.

Parkman told Deputy Ramsey, "New Jersey has enough to go forward. The big chiefs in Memphis might even say he's a suspect now." Parkman had waited two years for vindication of the jurisdiction dispute. With the exception of Memphis's homicide officers, the higher-ups didn't sound overjoyed, but he vowed to move on it with or without them.

Judging by the time lapse, the case was still a hard sell in Memphis. With irrefutable evidence and the prospect of more media embarrassment, the district attorney agreed to reopen the case and launch a joint probe with New Jersey.

Chapter 57
Detecting Lies

Monroe police got the word, "It's coming down, but keep it under wraps. We're trying to put an airtight case together." Memphis Detective Ken Carson contacted witnesses from two years before. Tara Hester found the timing ironic. "I was moving to Dallas and came across old pictures of Joel. Knowing Ivrin would be caught was a good close to that chapter of my life."

New Jersey needed to interview Ivrin's new girlfriend, Carolyn Buchner. Michael King, a master interrogator, could switch from *Kindergarten Cop* to *The Terminator* and Fitz-Patrick coaxed, "How about examining Buchner? We need you in."

"I don't hear a Hallelujah Chorus from Memphis. Fine, they're flying Detective Carson up tomorrow for the grand finale. We're doing a solo so they can wing-flap for the press."

He relented, "Okay, I'll interview her, but I'm not staying over tomorrow for an all-nighter. My kid has chicken pox and I haven't been home in two days."

Carolyn related her version of her romance with Ivrin and Michelle's behavior. King slid smoothly into the plan, "Could you have him contact us to clarify some facts before we can proceed with his complaint?"

Carson arrived in Mount Holly and the prosecutors briefed him, "We use the Meyers-Briggs technique called Kinesics Interviewing with amazing results."

Ready to roll, Captain Bob Scara, a veteran polygraphist, was in high spirits. He wore a tan cardigan and he hummed his lie detector theme song, "It's going to be a wonderful day today..."

Ivrin called the station. "Carolyn gave me your message. I can come in at 10:30." The staff recalled their training: *The tough guy routine is passé, no outmoded good-cop, bad-cop theatrics, yelling or intimidation. You're the unshockable listener helping the suspect transfer his feelings, thoughts and wishes over to you.*

Four detectives stood behind a two-way mirror to get a take on the suspect: $200 jogging suit, groomed, cool deportment, reading a newspaper as though bored, tapping his fingers on the chair's arm, a bit put upon by the wait. *Ah, so, not some freaked-out bum*, King probably thought. Textbook Kinesics flashed through his mind: *I only tell you that which you know. Enter the supernatural vision of the suspect through the doors of your own mind and look around. What is his fantasy, his driving force? What does he value, what would he kill for?*

Power, reputation, adoration. King told Fitz-Patrick, "Hey, I'm in! He should have brought an Atlantic City tip sheet and worn his jeans."

"Mr. Bolden," said King, "we need to clarify the information you gave in your first interview. About Miss Peterson checking up on you, what information did she hope to use against you?"

"I'd only spoken to her once about the Brenda Spicer case when she found the clipping. I didn't mention anything about Joel Tillis's death and I have no idea how she learned of it. She said she contacted the Memphis Police."

"Why do you think she did that?"

"I have no idea."

Forty-five minutes of innocuous questions passed, but then he must have realized that something else was happening. Fight or flight hit his brain—the trap mentality instead of a routine interview.

"Miss Peterson said you made admissions to her about the two murders? Did you in fact make those admissions?"

"No." He looked panicked.

"Are you willing to take a polygraph test to verify your denial regarding your admissions to her?"

"Yes." Legally, he was not a felon and to refuse would make him look guilty. He could beat their machine, Ivrin probably thought to himself.

Scara profiled him: Intelligent, shrewd, even-keeled and pretty much together. Showing some stress in his mannerisms. A touch of indignation as though offended. He had been there before, knew the routine. Scara used the polygraph technique developed for the Phoenix Police Department: *ask known truths and it normally invokes a reaction.* Designed to smoke out any other offenses on the suspect's mind, the brain hears trouble or bad news. If a person lies, the adrenaline fires and a change occurs.

"Did Michelle Peterson threaten to tell that you killed Joel Tillis?"

"Yes." *Response probably truthful,* Scara most likely noted.

"Did you ever tell her that you killed Joel Tillis?"

"No." Ivrin's reaction escalated.

"Is Peterson lying when she said you told her you killed Joel Tillis?"

"Yes." *Major reaction.*

"Did you kill Joel Tillis?"

"No." The needle drew Christmas trees on the chart.

"Were you acquitted of a murder in Louisiana?"

"Yes." *Major changes, deep concern over the acquittal.*

"Did you kill Brenda Spicer?"

"No." The graph registered wild changes.

On the second polygraph, because he knew what was coming and feared it, Ivrin's reactions increased. Scara studied the charts and told the detectives, "F-Minus. He blew out the wiring."

Ken Carson entered the room. A glint of curiosity crossed Ivrin's face:

they had switched cops. What happened to his advocates?

"Mr. Bolden," said King, "You failed your polygraphs."

Carson introduced himself, "I'm with the Memphis Police Department."

Ivrin stared morosely. He was screwed. "If I have to go through all that again, I guess I will. What's going to happen to me? Am I being arrested?"

"In no way are you being detained or arrested," said King. "You're free to leave at any time. Or you can voluntarily remain and continue the interview." Five hours had passed. The cliffhanger could go either way. Detectives held their breaths. Only the drone of the fluorescent light was heard.

"I'll stay." Their reasonable, non-judgmental voices, the room an inferno without an escape, *Get it out. Get rid of it.* "We did argue that day over the car. The one we owned jointly was the only car in operation."

Ivrin stopped, "What's going to happen to the person who killed her?"

King said, "I can't advise you what would happen to the person responsible for Miss Tillis's death since the circumstances aren't known at this time. The details could possibly determine if it was accidental or intentional. In no way do I encourage you to say this was an accident just to minimize it."

Ivrin studied the floor. Could he be wondering if he could claim it was an accident? She pushed him to mad mad mad. The room spun. A loner in a city without connections—was he sick of competing, sick of devious women, sick of cops or just sick of being on the run?

The room was pin-drop quiet. Finally, he broke the silence. "I'll tell you how it happened." He caved in and broke down crying. Weeping for himself, the purging took two more hours. "We'd been arguing for a week, not really speaking. It was verbal, then physical. She said 'I've already got somebody else I'm leaving you for.' She was cursing me, threatening me with another guy. Always before, she got me up to a point and that was it. I strangled her. She was gasping and stopped breathing. I drove to Arkansas and dumped her. Then I disposed of her work shirt and items that would identify her in a trash bin behind a tire store in Memphis."

He denied knowing anything about a diary or computer disks. "Do you own a computer?" asked King.

"Yes. But my floppy disks were taken in the burglary."

The detectives locked eyes. Peterson and her buddy had probably sent the tell-all disk to its burial in the city landfill.

Certain that Peterson had been next on the hit list, King asked, "How did you come about making the admissions to Michelle Peterson that you had killed two women before?"

"She and I had argued. I took her home to her mother's so I could think about things. I didn't want to chance physically harming her. I told her about the murders so she'd understand why we couldn't be together."

King pressed his advantage. "Other than Joel Tillis, who was the other girl you killed?"

"Brenda Spicer." Carson suppressed his astonishment. Behind the two-way mirror Fitz-Patrick whispered, "Two royal flushes."

"What were the circumstances of her death?"

Ivrin became incoherent, "I don't know; she made me mad too. I was…always wanted to be whatever girl, having attention without others around. I tried talking to Brenda and Joel about it, but they kept on. At my storage locker, I was just trying to talk to Brenda Spicer, but she said she was going to be with Joel no matter what. So I strangled her, put her in a dumpster and returned to the game." He didn't mention the rape and sodomy.

When he reached his mother, King heard him say, "I'm arrested for killing Joel."

He phoned Carolyn who listened in bewildered silence. On his car, which was seized in the parking lot, a faded honors fraternity window sticker curled at the edges.

Chapter 58

True Confessions

Fitz-Patrick called Parkman, "We have a confession. He told us everything. Before we can arrest him, Memphis has to formally advise us he's wanted there and fax a warrant. Then we can take an affidavit from our end."

Detective Carson called Memphis, "We've got his confession on the Tillis case, plus a bonus. He also admitted to Spicer in Louisiana. We couldn't shut him up."

"Okay," his supervisor said, "I'll contact the county attorney general and have them send what you need." Hovering near the fax machine, Minervino, Fitz-Patrick and King drank too much coffee. Bolden could have still walked out at any time. "You believe this? What's taking them so long? I thought everything was on go."

Two hours elapsed before Memphis prosecutors called back to advise Carson that charges would be initiated. "The arrest warrant's being typed and we'll have to get a judge's approval." Five hours after the confessions, the fax finally delivered the arrest warrant and Carson said at last, "You're under arrest for the first-degree murder of Joel Tillis. You'll be incarcerated here pending extradition to Memphis."

Ivrin signed a waiver and King told Carson, "I strongly advise you to take him and run before he waffles. We can arrange it with the airlines for tomorrow morning."

"I'll have to check with my superiors." Permission denied. "He'll be extradited according to standard procedure. We'll get someone from the Sheriff's Department Fugitive Squad to fly up there and accompany you and the defendant back."

The detectives, whipped from exhaustion, were dumbfounded. "Are we making wine here? Nothing taken until it's time? They should ditch their rulebook and let Carson take him on the next flight out."

Two days later, the Fugitive Squad flew in but returned to Memphis empty-handed. Ivrin's parents had contacted an attorney famous for defending a man accused of the hired murder of his wife. He used the lag time well.

Mount Holly prosecutors' qualms materialized, "Bolden's jack-knifed. If he gets out, he's out of the country." His new defense attorney said his client had changed his mind about voluntary extradition and convinced a judge to dismiss the waiver.

In Monroe, Causey paged Peel, "What would be the best news you could hear about a former client?"

"That Ivrin Bolden's been arrested. If I can't have that, I'll take the lottery."

"You got it. New Jersey jailed him on first degree. He failed his polygraph and confessed to both the Spicer and Tillis murders. Even if he recants and hires six lawyers this time around, they've got him."

A fellow detective picked up curious vibes. Nothing came from the executive offices and Causey was unusually quiet. He asked, "Bill, don't you think you'd better tell the chief about this? If he hears it on the street, he'll probably be embarrassed." And infuriated.

Ivrin, by some adversarial right, belonged to Causey and Ivrin's downfall seemed anticlimatic. It was the worst case of Causey's career and he didn't relish slinking into the chief's office tooting New Jersey's horn. He called Carson in Memphis. "Congratulations, man. We're elated. Anybody who could fold him is a genius."

The twists seemed endless. A police officer friend had recently tipped me that Ivrin had applied for a gun permit in New Jersey—then I heard nothing. I doubted my sanity for having responded to Brenda Spicer's picture in the newspaper five years before when I had picked up on duplicity beneath the spin. If truth was such a virtue, why did so many fear it?

My roots were showing and I wore the same jeans for three days. Beyond the blue screen of words was the bayou's serenity and I was trapped inside, going nowhere. Not a watcher of daytime television, some mysterious instinct that had often pointed the way told me to take a break and I decided to watch the Oprah Winfrey Show.

Suddenly, a breaking news bulletin: "Ivrin Bolden was arrested today in New Jersey and charged with the murder of Joel Tillis in Memphis."

My telephone didn't stop ringing for days.

At Northeast Louisiana University, Adminstrator Paul Bannon heard the news and closed his eyes. He loved Joel as a sister. The mountain of debts to the devil had been paid off. At the University Police Department, Chief Ellerman told Ed Free, "You can quit kicking yourself with what-ifs. With the confession maybe he could be charged with the aggravated rape of Spicer since it wasn't included in the murder indictment here."

As the cameras rolled, Memphis claimed the case and the credit, "A murder case is never closed. We reopened it after finding new evidence linking Bolden to the murder. Every time we get more information, we're able to put pieces together." Sheriff Parkman could go spelunking. He and New Jersey weren't mentioned.

In Arkansas, Deputy Ramsey, a songwriter and guitarist, snorted, "Reminds me of that country song, 'You take the bows; I'll take the blame.'"

Not this time, slickers." The press, who smelled Memphis PR again, lit up the lines to Forrest City. Relieved of the body he had carried for over two years, Parkman said, "New Jersey contacted us first. We both convinced Memphis to reopen the case."

New Jersey prosecutors would have be the next to continue working on solving the case—a brilliant effort just beginning. Over the next five months, they bore the $30,000 expense of four court hearings defending the extradition against a grand scale effort by Ivrin's attorney to discover the evidence and hold more hearings on the domestic problems and the charges against Michelle Peterson. By law, Ivrin wasn't entitled to the hearings. Memphis had all they needed to extradite: Charge pending, an indictment, subject identified as person wanted and proof he was in Memphis at the time.

Ivrin, smart and aggressive, looked complacent throughout each court proceeding. His defense attorney raised the issue, "The prosecution needs to show Joel Tillis was killed in between certain days." Court was recessed and Assistant District Attorney Minevero raced to call Memphis police for confirmation.

After work, King, Fitz-Patrick, Minevero and other staffers gathered at a local tavern in their tradition of "A Case for a Case"—beers and summing up—minus their usual boisterous toasts. They hadn't solved the enigma of Ivrin's uncanny effect on women. Carolyn believed he was innocent, still loved him and visited him in jail.

Chapter 59

Searching for Answers

My journey wouldn't be finished until the enigma in Memphis ended with prosecution or an anticipated plea bargain. I needed to convince Detective Ed Perrino to allow me to come to New Jersey. Tossing my messages aside, he figured me for another newshound. Finally, he took my call and my Southern drawl wore him down. "I don't have time to chase around and check you out. Send me your spiel and I'll bounce it off the county."

I also had to convince a fast-track prosecutor's office to trust me. "So far away, you can't fully appreciate what you accomplished. These were high profile cases affecting many lives, careers and institutions. You wrapped up two notorious murders, not yours to solve, but nobody's strewing palm branches."

King and Fitz-Patrick conferred with Prosecutor Raymond. "She sounds credible, but is she on the level? Maybe she's a plant hired by Bolden's attorney to deliver evidence they didn't get at the extradition hearings."

They contacted Detective Carson in Memphis, "Naaw. She's a writer who's followed the cases from square one."

King laughed, "We're disappointed. We were going to buy trench coats, wear dark glasses and leave copies of spy magazines lying around."

Detective Perrino went soft. "Hotels are expensive; you can stay with me and my wife. Burlington County is sprawled out and you'll need transportation. And you'd probably be mugged before leaving Philly, so we'll meet you at Union Station. How do I pick you out of the crowd?"

"I'll be wearing a tan coat with a brown scarf."

"And I'm a little Italian about five-foot-eight."

Something got lost in the translation and Perrino's wife laughed nervously, "Ed, a kerchief? They went out with bloomers. Maybe they still say kerchief in the South."

The Perrinos browsed for a country bumpkin. A huge woman in a tan coat bounced off the escalator and Ed said, "If that's her, I'm leaving. We don't have enough food in the house." *After ten minutes, a stylish anorexic beauty strolled in their direction and his wife warned,* "If that's her, we're both leaving." *I paged them and relief flooded their faces: I was somewhere in between their apprehensions.*

On Prosecutor Raymond's desk a plaque read, "Achieve a record worthy of publicity, then call in the press."

I gawked at King, sharply dressed in a navy suit and filling the doorway with iron-pumping physique. "No need to embellish you guys."

He laughed, "What was your vision? Dweebs in polyester?"

Fitz-Patrick spoke of divine intervention, the prayer of every inventive cop, the so-called coincidence of the gun permit application and the burglary charge against Peterson which led them to Ivrin Bolden. "That's when the intercession becomes evidence."

In the eight months since Ivrin's extradition, the police moved on to new cases. They hadn't expected Memphis to throw a parade, nor had they received a single message of thanks or congratulations from Louisiana. Normally, Southern courtesy was as inborn as baking a pecan pie for new neighbors. I felt ashamed.

Michelle Peterson agreed to meet at a cafe. I found Michelle attractive with a dispirited expression. She asked the inevitable, "Why did you choose this subject?"

"Geography in the beginning. The first murder happened in my hometown and gave me access. Then it mushroomed on its own."

Closely I met her eyes. "When you came forward and cooperated with the police, you probably saved your own life and possibly the lives of other women."

Yes, she did believe Ivrin had planned to kill her. The clairvoyant who read her Tarot cards regularly told her all about it. "He kept trying to get me back to his apartment again so we could talk. My family warned me not to go. I think he would have done me in, too. I don't think he moved here because of me. How much do you know about his life in Florida?"

"Some."

As we said goodbye, she was pensive, "I guess Ivrin's mad at me for turning him in."

"Maybe he wanted to get caught."

"That's what my mother said, too." *I watched her leave. There but for luck went a dead woman.*

When I returned home, I heard that prosecution witness Benjamin Potter was living in New Orleans and I tracked him down to fill in a few blanks. He suggested meeting at a quaint but elegant restaurant. Most of what he told me I already knew, but he shared one thing. Though he'd left after testifying, he now told why, "I intimidated Ivrin; he was afraid of me and jealous, because I dated Joel while he was in med school."

The next morning it was time to leave. Crossing the Pontchartrain Causeway, I knew that like a messenger to the dead, I had to detour through Jena. In the cemetery, a dove of peace and a basketball free shot resembling a rainbow were chiseled in marble: "Spicer…Her Zest for Life Lives On." *A bouquet of wildflowers tied with colorful ribbons trailed from the top of the headstone.*

Chapter 60

Double Jeopardy

Ivrin was expected to be convicted of Joel's death, but Monroe wanted justice for Spicer. The new District Attorney Jerry Jones pointed out, "The double jeopardy clause in the constitution prevents him from retrial on the first murder. Maybe we could charge him with violating Brenda Spicer's civil rights." Hard to prove and hopefully unnecessary, for all felt certain that Memphis prosecutors would give him a long sentence for Tillis's murder.

Joel's mother told reporters, "I'm relieved the wheels of justice are still turning. It's hard to express my emotions when the Memphis police told me they *may* have the man who killed my daughter in custody. That the man *might be Ivrin*. If he did this, I feel betrayed."

The interview closed by saying, "She testified on his behalf at his trial for the murder of Brenda Spicer."

The Spicers gave a statement, "We don't understand a justice system which allows defendants more than one opportunity for appeal, but only one chance for conviction. A couple of years ago, we had to accept that judicial efforts had failed. Perhaps nothing would ever be done. We turned it over to the Higher Court and He took care of it."

Lunching with his wife, Administrator Paul Bannon saw a professor who was a character witness at Ivrin's trial. "Well, what do you think about his arrest?"

He pulled up a chair, "Well, if they say he did it and he confessed, I guess he did. But I never believed it."

"You didn't find him a little strange? I sure did," Bannon said.

"Well, I do recall giving him a grade he didn't want and he got upset. He waited for me after class and followed me home."

"That didn't bother you? If a student tried to intimidate me, I'd pull him from his car and beat the crap out of him."

"Yeah, I guess, looking back." He left and Bannon's wife said, "That would have made a better story in court. Was everybody afraid of him?"

Spring rolled into summer with Ivrin's extradition from New Jersey back to Memphis postponed repeatedly. Prosecutors hung in, amazed when the Boldens shelled out over $25,000 to fight it. After four months in jail, the Memphis Fugitive Squad escorted him from the plane. The DA's office, hostile before, had invited the media. Wearing a jogging suit, hands wrapped in white to hide his handcuffs, Ivrin glanced quizzically at the unexpected reception.

He was incarcerated for six more months, but nothing moved on the case except more postponements. To some it appeared as if Memphis hoped to avoid a costly first-degree trial and put the mortifying case to rest without a media splash.

Whatever the reason, a high stakes poker game played out. In an unscheduled hearing behind closed doors, Ivrin was allowed to plead to involuntary manslaughter—under a statute carrying no admission of guilt. He was sentenced immediately to ten years with his jail time credited; he could be eligible for parole in four-and-one-half years. The rationale was, "The victim and the defendant were fighting on the day of her murder. With all emotions set aside, the evidence fits the category of accidental death."

The news jolted Monroe. Five years of waiting had ended with what seemed to some like a wrist slap and a whimper.

I was curious to know what the New Jersey Police thought of the sentence. Since Ivrin's extradition, they had heard nothing and my update stunned them. After monumental money and manpower spent on a case not theirs, surely they would have been notified of the results.

Fitz-Patrick and King mulled it over. "Writers tend to exaggerate. If she's correct, what could have gone wrong? He confessed. Involuntary manslaughter after all our sweat? There must be a logical explanation, some legal snafu."

Fitz-Patrick telephoned the Memphis DA's office. "I don't have to explain anything to you," he was told.

Then he called me back, "Tell us what's going on down there. I got a total freeze out. Memphis wouldn't even discuss it."

I could only send the press coverage and my opinion, "No else understood it, either."

Chapter 61

Outcry

A Monroe newspaper polled public reaction: "Was justice served in the plea bargain and sentencing of Ivrin Bolden?" Two hundred and fifty-one people said "No." Fourteen said "Yes." Angry letters flooded the editor:

"My cousin got ten years for beating up his girlfriend. Bolden killed two women and got the same sentence."

"Mike Tyson got that on a rape conviction."

"Justice served itself. Joel Tillis knew what he did and still backed him up."

"Justice is for the rich and powerful. Our legal system is a joke."

Old wounds were salted that only retribution could heal. District Attorney Jerry Jones asked a court reporter, "How long would it take you to type a transcript of the Bolden trial?"

Divine Intercession again—a motion to erase the proceedings under the rules of an acquittal had never been filed and the Guardian of the Tapes still had them. "I've already typed a transcript. The lady writing a book about the cases hired me." Jones sent a deputy to my home to borrow the only copy.

He flipped through the transcript and tapped a finger on the line he was looking for. "Here it is. He said under oath, 'No, I did not kill Brenda Spicer,' then confessed to New Jersey that he did. Perjury is better than nothing."

He filed an immediate arrest warrant and extradition back to Monroe. Memphis responded faster than usual. After sixteen months in the Tennessee Reception Center, Ivrin felt incarceration close to home, with access to his family and their lawyers, was more acceptable. His new attorney argued the perjury charge bordered on double jeopardy, a retrial of the Spicer case. The court ruled against him.

Judge Michael Ingram appointed me foreperson of the District Court Grand Jury. After hearing cases, we were responsible for touring and inspecting penal facilities and submitting a report. We were curious about the courthouse's star resident. The jail commander described Ivrin Bolden as a model prisoner and opened the cellblock where he shared a miniscule space with three other men. Smiling broadly with a sweeping bow, he said, "Come into my suite." *The friendliest, most normal-looking killer one could imagine seemed unworried. Thankfully, he didn't recognize me.*

Chapter 62
Circular Endings

Five years after Brenda Spicer's murder, Ivrin Bolden went on trial for lying on the stand. A change of venue was allowed, because of extensive publicity in Monroe. Law enforcement officers from Tennessee, Arkansas and New Jersey who had pursued the same man met for the first time at the Alexandria, Louisiana, courthouse.

District Attorney Jerry Jones, his chief prosecutor Chuck Cook and Assistant DA Mike Ruddick had put months and mega-bucks into a mere perjury trial to correct the mistakes of the past and safeguard other potential victims. The supposedly simple issue of whether Ivrin Bolden had lied under oath required intense preparation, sound judiciary arguments and subtle presentation. They walked a legal high wire and one misstep into the forbidden area of whether Bolden *killed* Spicer constituted double jeopardy. Staying with what he had *said* was a formidable challenge. Joel Tillis's murder was irrelevant to the perjury charge and jurors had to judge whether Bolden was a liar rather than a repeat killer.

Defense Attorney Marty Stroud, another heavy hitter, gave it his best argument: his client had not been sufficiently informed of his Miranda, not allowed access to a lawyer and claimed New Jersey detectives used false pretenses to coerce the confession.

Examining the defendant, DA Jones smiled wryly, "So all these police officers testifying here today are lying?"

"Yes." Laughing involuntarily, Ivrin ducked his head.

Jones bristled, "Everyone's always picking on you aren't they, Ivrin?"

Monroe Police Detective Jim Gregory stood in for Detective Bill Causey, who had lost his valiant two-year battle with cancer at age forty-five before seeing the conclusion of the murder case he had investigated for so long. Ivrin showed no emotion during the three-day trial until Joel's mother was mentioned and then he looked sad and upset. The mother figure who had welcomed him into her home seemed the only person capable of eliciting his remorse.

In a reversal of roles to shore up the claim that New Jersey detectives had denied Ivrin access to his lawyer, his former attorney Edwin Greer testified on Ivrin's behalf. Producing a two-year-old $500 invoice he claimed was payment to a Memphis attorney for ongoing representation, Greer grew visibly annoyed by Chuck Cook questioning his veracity. Dismissed from testimony, he and his paralegal exited the courthouse.

The bare-bones issue of perjury went to the jury. Two hours inched by with intense arguing escaping the deliberation room. Spectators, witnesses and police officers paced and visited, shared gum and vending machine snacks. Unnerved by waiting, some voiced the unthinkable, "Dear God, he's going to walk again."

Finally, the jury returned their unanimous verdict, "We find the defendant guilty as charged." Ivrin showed no reaction to the maximum ten-year sentence to run concurrently with his ten-year plea bargain in Memphis.

Detectives Michael King and Scott Fitz-Patrick, impressed by prosecutors Jones, Cook and Ruddick, left Louisiana with a kinder view of Southern law enforcement.